G000256750

The U

David Farr is a writer and director. His plays *The Danny Crowe Show*, *Elton John's Glasses* and *Night of the Soul* have all been published by Faber, who have also published his collected *Plays One*. As Joint Artistic Director of Bristol Old Vic (2003–5) he has directed *Paradise Lost* by John Milton, *The Odyssey* by Homer and Shakespeare's *A Midsummer Night's Dream*, *The Comedy of Errors* and *Twelfth Night*. He has directed *Coriolanus* and *Julius Caesar* for the RSC, was Artistic Director of London's Gate Theatre from 1995 to 1998, and is now Artistic Director of the Lyric Theatre, Hammersmith. *The UN Inspector* opened at the National Theatre in June 2005.

DAVID FARR

The UN Inspector

freely adapted from
The Government Inspector
by Nikolai Gogol

faber and faber

First published in 2005
by Faber and Faber Limited
3 Queen Square, London WC1N 3AU

Typeset by Country Setting, Kingsdown, Kent CT14 8ES
Printed in England by Mackays of Chatham plc, Chatham, Kent

A CIP record for this book
is available from the British Library

ISBN 0–571–22899–2

2 4 6 8 10 9 7 5 3 1

This play is dedicated to the memory
of the anti-government journalist

Georgi Gongadze

whose headless body was found
in the year 2000 in the Ukraine

*With thanks to Patrick Marber, Nicholas Hytner,
Tom Morris, Mark Ravenhill, Carey Scott,
Rachel Lomax, Patrick, Tom and Gavin
at Global Witness and Anne Siddons*

and Nikolai Gogol

The UN Inspector was first performed in the Olivier auditorium of the National Theatre, London, on 7 June 2005. The cast was as follows:

The President Kenneth Cranham
Minister for Justice David Ryall
Minister for Health Michael Gould
Minister for Education Sam Cox
Minister for Finance Elizabeth Bell
Head of Intelligence Geoffrey Beevers
Peter Robchinski Justin Salinger
Peter Dobchinski Jonathan McGuinness
Svistunov Mark Leadbetter
Anna Andreyevna Geraldine James
Maria Antonovna Daisy Haggard
Horst Gibner Tony Turner
Sammy Nicolas Tennant
Martin Gammon Michael Sheen
Waiter Nick Fletcher
Michka Mark Arends
Security Man Nicholas Tizzard
Businessmen Cornelius Booth, Peter Aubrey
Mother Penelope McGhie
Activist Michelle Dockery
Aide Kate Best

Director David Farr
Designer Ti Green
Lighting Designer Mark Henderson
Music Keith Clouston
Sound Designer John Leonard
Company Voice Work Patsy Rodenburg
Assistant Director Hanna Berrigan

Characters

Anton Antonovich Skvosnik
President, around fifty-five.
An ex-Soviet bigwig who has remodelled himself
and has served constantly as president for fifteen years

Luka Klopov
Minister for Education, fifty. A devoted family man
and another member of the Soviet nomenklatura. Tall

Stepana Ivanovna Korobkin
Minister of Finance, fifty, female.
A wily, experienced, canny operator with strong
Soviet connections. Ex-KGB

Georgy Zemlyanika
Minister for Health, forty-five. An ex-industrialist,
a constant smoker and in with the Americans

Ammos Lyapkin
Minister of Justice and Internal Security, fifty-eight.
A corpulent patriot, happy to follow any orders

Ivan Kuzmich Sphyokin
Head of Intelligence, fifty. A born optimist, happy
to pursue any avenues, legal or illegal, in search of
interesting information

Peter Dobchinski
Government Aide, twenty-eight, with Mafia connections

Peter Robchinski
Government Aide, thirty, with Mafia connections

Horst Gibner
A World Bank delegate and economist, German

Anna Andreyevna
Wife of the President, approaching fifty

Maria Antonovna
Daughter of the President, eighteen

Svistunov
Head of the President's personal security operation.
Ex-KGB

A Waiter
at the Marriott Hotel

Michka
A house servant in the presidential residence

Female Activist

Mother
of a missing journalist

Martin Gammon
A young British businessman with big dreams
and small pockets

Sammy
His loyal friend

A delegation of small businessmen

Various bodyguards, security personnel, militia,
doctors, politicians and their wives

THE UN INSPECTOR

freely adapted by David Farr from
Nikolai Gogol's *The Government Inspector*

Act One

*A huge room in the President's residence. Signs of the old
Soviet regime, long pulled down and replaced by images
of the new West. Ceremonial double doors. Huge bay
windows. Smaller single doors to left and right. Nine
o'clock in the morning.*

*Enter the Minister for Health through the double doors
with a Big Mac and fries. Takes out cigarette. Smokes.
Puts out. Eats.*
    *An Aide runs across with a tray of Starbucks' coffees.
Another Aide runs across on the phone.*

Aide The President needs the Minister of Finance here
now . . . Then wake her up . . . Tell her it's a disaster. Tell
her to get in contact with the regional office of the World
Bank . . . She needs to bring Herr Gibner over here . . .

    Exit Aide. Enter the Ministers of Justice and Education.

Justice What do you know, Georgy?

Health It's UN.

Education UN what?

Health Inspectors.

Education Oh shit!

Justice How do we know?

Health The President got a call from a friend in the US.
We're waiting for an email to get more information.

Education But they're coming here?

Health Looks like it.

3

Education Shit! When?

Health They haven't announced it yet. Stop trembling, Luka, and have a chip.

Education I can't eat fast food now. We need to think.

Health It's the UN, Luka. You have time for a French fry.

Justice But why would they pick on us? We're an emerging democracy. We've turned our back on the Soviet system. We've liberalised. We've opened barriers to trade. We've followed the IMF guidelines to the letter.

Enter Minister of Finance, still trying to arrange her hair.

Finance What is it?

Justice UN.

Education Inspectors.

Finance When are they coming? I have to call the Exchequer. They need to turn on the shredders.

Health Will everyone stop panicking!

Enter the President, fast, and accompanied by Security, who guard the doors.

All Mr President!

President Gentlemen. I have some very unpleasant news.

Health We know.

Finance UN.

Education Inspectors.

President I knew something was up. I had a dream last night. There were these rats, giant blue rats, sniffing round my sleeping body, sniffing, sniffing.

Health Mr President, if I may. At the moment it's just a rumour. It needs to turn into an intention, then into a resolution. There'll be amendments, vetoes. That's the great thing about the UN. They always give you time to prepare.

President Not any more, Georgy. (*Beat.*) I have the email. It was sent to me by a cousin of mine who works in corporate intelligence in Baltimore. This is what he says: 'Dearest friend, colleague and comrade . . .' Hold on . . . here we are . . . 'Feel it my duty to inform you that a top UN official has arrived in your neck of the woods with instructions to investigate rumours of government corruption, electoral fraud and humanitarian abuses. Have this from the most reliable of sources. Now as I know you're human like the rest of us and may in the undertaking of government business have lined the odd pocket' – well we're all friends here – 'you should know that he is passing himself off as an ordinary traveller. Take a special care. He may be with you at any time. He may have arrived already and is most likely staying under an assumed name at one of the new international hotels. As for me, I spent a pleasant afternoon with Uncle Andrei and Auntie Olga feeding the ducks in Central Park and listening to Auntie playing the violin. How she connects with Rachmaninov . . .' Well, I can read that later. So, gentlemen, there you have it.

Minister of Health lights up a cigarette.

Finance Here already.

Education Under cover. An assumed name. Oh God.

President It appears the UN is starting to show its teeth.

Justice Then we should knock them out! I mean to say. We're not some tinpot dictatorship. In . . . what's it called? I've got it in my bag, here we are. (*He brandishes* *a copy of* Newsweek.) 'A model of free-market capitalism in the post-Soviet era'. We've got friends in high places! Minister of Finance! (*to Finance*) Where's our World Bank delegate? The little Kraut with the face like a toad. What's his name?

Finance I brought Herr Gibner with me. He's waiting outside.

Justice Well, bring him in.

Finance I ought to warn you he's not at his best . . .

Justice Just bring him in. Bring him in.

Stepana exits.

He can call his head office in Washington. Tell those UN pricks to learn some manners. Mark my words, this 'inspection' will be over by lunch time.

Gibner enters clutching a globe.

Ah, Herr Gibner, there you are! What does the World Bank have to say about these UN upstarts? You guys can put a stop to this, can't you?

Pause. Gibner giggles.

President Herr Gibner? This is a situation of some urgency, and as our World Bank delegate we should be glad of your input.

Gibner giggles again and spins his globe. The ministers all look at each other.

Gibner (*German accent*) And the mountain shall fall into the sea, and the shibboleths crumble before his mighty wrath. And the city of greed and lust shall lie in waste like the land of dead souls.

Pause.

Health What did he say?

6

Finance (*confidentially*) His office say he received a phone call from America last night. His face went pale and he started weeping. I found him in the gutter outside his mansion holding that child's globe and muttering, 'This is my punishment'

Gibner The party's over, gentlemen. They're coming to get us!

He stares at them and giggles.

Health What about the IMF? Can't they put a stop to it?

President I called their offices in Washington. They said they support the UN in all its investigations.

Justice My arse they do. The last IMF commission that came here gave me a Kofi Annan dartboard.

Finance Did you try Moscow? The private line?

President I was told no one was available to take my call.

Finance So who answered the phone?

President I was told no one was available to tell me. (*Beat.*) We're on our own, gentlemen.

Beat. Minister of Justice pours himself a drink.

Education So what if he is coming? I mean, we've got nothing to hide, have we? Let him come, that's what I say!

President The Minister for Education is in very bullish mood this morning. But if he took time to visit the schools he is ministering he might not be so defiant.

Education I visit schools. I took my children just this morning.

President Luka, your children's school is in the most fashionable area of the city. But what about the schools elsewhere? What about the North?

Education There aren't any schools in the North.

President Precisely!

Finance But he won't go to the North. (*Beat.*) He can't go to the North.

President Why else would he be here?

Health Oh no, he can't. We can't let him. We've been turning a blind eye until it calms down. He needs to know that.

President And what about the families coming here to escape the trouble? The slums building up all over the city?

Health But this is a recent problem . . . We need time to take the measures necessary to deal with such an influx . . .

President Has anyone been to see the extent of the problem?

Education I have. I pass them on my way to the spa.

Justice When are they going to finish that damned jacuzzi?

President Can we please focus on the fucking slums?

Education Conditions don't look all that bad through the windscreen.

President But this is what I mean. Why would an inspector be here unless he wanted to see the conditions in the poorest areas? We're a small country, we've avoided the media spotlight. Our own television, though strictly independent of course . . .

All Of course.

President . . . is sensitive in its treatment of these issues, it understands we need more time to resolve the humanitarian tensions in certain areas. But if this gets out . . . We need some good-news stories. Draw his attention away. Where are Robchinski and Dobchinski?

Justice They went to the Marriott to brainstorm your speech on national security.

President They went to the Marriott to get a decent cappuccino. They're my aides, they should be aiding me! Minister for Health!

Health (*puffing away*) Yes, Mr President!

President The new hospital in Brezhnev Park –

Health You mean Liberty Park.

President Yes, Liberty Park. I want that hospital opened. We've been waiting too long as it is.

Health Mr President, I need to report a few teething problems.

President Teething problems?

Health The private consortium are suing us for misleading them in the formation of the contract. Typical bloody French.

President Which means?

Health Which means the construction team are off-site. The building is there, but there are some missing elements.

President What elements?

Health Ventilation, electricity and water are the biggest hurdles. And internal walls.

Justice But I don't understand – I drove by the hospital on my way to the ski slopes. I saw spanking new ambulances, doctors in immaculate white coats ferrying the injured into A and E, beautiful young nurses caring for the distressed with shy smiles and a delicate touch.

Health Well, that's a tricky one. You see the building's just standing there while all this is sorted out, so I thought, to make a bit of money, well – you know the soap opera *Ambulance Division*?

President The one set in the A and E Department? Yes, of course, my wife loves it. Great production values.

Pause.

Georgy, you're not saying . . .? Georgy, this is a two-hundred-million-dollar hospital funded by banks from twelve countries. You're not using it as a . . .?

Health Temporarily.

President Stop it! Get them out! Today!

Health Can I wait until tomorrow? They're shooting the second part of the 'blind girl under a bus' episode. It's rather moving.

President Someone tell me some good news.

Justice (*proudly*) The prisons are full of one hundred per cent bona fide wrongdoers. Not an actor amongst them.

President But what about the overcrowding? Last time I tried to make a visit I couldn't get in.

Justice It's all the protest marches about the election. We're running short on capacity.

President Well, release some. Call it an amnesty.

Justice They'll only start marching again. They're addicted to it.

President Well, release the thieves and the fraudsters. We can pick them up again when he's gone. Now then, where else can he screw us? We need to examine every area. (*He searches frantically.*) Where is it? Where is it? Ah here we are. (*He takes out an enormous document.*)

Structural adjustment loan from International Monetary Fund . . . Loan of six hundred million US dollars . . . repayable at four . . . bla bla bla . . . here we are! Conditions of loan. Let's see how we're doing. Condition one. The privatisation of all public utilities.

All (*triumphantly*) Achieved!

President To be sold by international tender, ensuring fair and free competition and the preservation of key assets.

All (*less triumphantly*) Ah.

President Who did we sell the water board to?

Finance Your cousin Dmitri.

President And the gas?

Finance Was sold to Georgy's nephew.

President What's he doing with it?

Health He stripped the assets and sold it to a Texan conglomerate. They're making a mint.

President How are they making a mint?

Health Doubling prices and being more selective about distribution.

President Meaning?

Finance The North's been cut off for three months.

President What about the electricity?

Finance The electricity supply went to Luka's daughter.

Education (*proudly*) It was a sixteenth-birthday present.

All (*except the President and Finance*) Aaaah, bless.

President What the hell do you think you're playing at!

Luka, tell your daughter to sell up immediately. You can't be in pigtails and own the national grid. Let's go on. Condition two: free and fair elections.

Herr Gibner giggles.

Why did he laugh when I said free and fair elections?

Herr Gibner laughs.

He did it again. What do you mean by that, you little . . .? Get him out of here. My father fought at Stalingrad, mate, he ate nothing but snow and worms for six months, so don't you talk to me about democracy!

Exit Gibner, escorted by officials.

The elections were perfectly free! I was free to vote, weren't you, Ammos?

Justice Free as a bird, Mr President.

Education My polling station was an oasis of democracy.

President We even had international monitors, didn't we?

Justice They were Danish.

Health I seem to recall they focused their attentions on the beach resorts in the south.

Justice Yes, we gave them gorgeous sea-view apartments. They said the windsurfing was fantastic. And the instructors I got weren't bad either. (*He laughs.*) Didn't know the first thing about windsurfing! (*He laughs.*) Not bad at all!

President (*interrupting*) Condition three: the closure of the unprofitable chemical plants in the inaccessible North of the country.

All Achieved!

President And the creation of a benefits system and transport infrastructure to cater for the high level of unemployment and population displacement caused by these closures.

All Ah.

President Did we not create a system of social benefits?

Pause.

Nor a transport infrastructure?

Pause.

But this is dreadful. We must build a road to the North today. And we must start a wonderful benefits system!

Health Mr President, a comprehensive benefits system would cost millions!

President That's why they loaned us hundreds of millions! If the inspector reports that we have been abusing our responsibilities, the IMF will be forced to postpone the next tranche of the loan. Do you have any idea what that means?

Finance No more private jets for the First Lady?

President It means global shame. We'll have to renege on our debt payments. They'll call in the auditors. Nasty Belgian men in grey suits encamped in this palace. Searching through my affairs with their mousy little hands and handlebar moustaches. They'll bring down the lot of us. Turf us out on the street and let the mob loose on us. Our bank accounts will be frozen. We'll have to hide away in unheated bungalows on state pensions. Stones thrown at our windows. Dog poo poured through our letter boxes. Our dream of dining at the top table dashed. Myself and Anna Andreyevna never to sit sipping tea on the lawn of the Rose Garden with George and Laura before indulging in a light supper of chilli beef, French fries and lashings of . . . what I mean to say is we need a clean up! Minister of Education, I want an immediate new drive. A desk for every child in the North. With their name on it.

Education But where do we put them?

President I don't know! Stick them on a hill. High-altitude schooling. Say it's a Dutch idea.

Education They don't have hills.

President Minister of Justice, empty your prisons of the thieves and killers. Minister of Health, get that TV crew out of the hospital! Build some walls! Get electricity! And Minister of Finance, you and I need to find a few million in handouts to the poor. If we announce it today, the timing could be perfect. Unless of course he's already here! He'll suddenly appear and say, 'Ah, here you are, my pretties. Mr President, Mr Minister of Justice, Ms Finance, Mr Health. Step forward! Step forward and explain yourselves!'

Enter the Head of Intelligence.

Intelligence Hello, everyone, what's all this about a secret UN Inspector ?

All Sssshhhh!

President You mean you've already heard?

Intelligence (*proudly*) I am the Head of Intelligence. Of course I heard.

President How?

Intelligence One of your aides told me. Peter Dobchinski. Or was it Peter Robchinski? They were on their way to the Marriott to grab a latte. Don't worry, I've been keeping it very hush-hush.

President Well, what do you think?

Pause as the Head of Intelligence is flummoxed.

Come on, tell me . . . As my Head of Intelligence . . .
what do you really think Ivan?

Intelligence Me. Well. As your Head of Intelligence . . .
(*Beat.*) What do you really think, Anton?

President Well, it's not that I'm afraid. I'm just concerned
that some of the small businessmen, companies, individuals
– well everyone, really. Ivan this might sound like a
return to the bad old days, but could you quietly check
all the post going out of the country? And maybe have
a quick look at the emails as well. Just to check if they
contain any attacks on me. I'm sure most will be quite
innocent. But just in case.

Intelligence To be honest, I do it anyway, out of curiosity.
It's fun finding out what's new in people's lives.

President But has anyone mentioned a UN official? Or
maybe someone from New York?

Intelligence No. Nothing from New York at all. A couple
from Moscow describing the sex-club scene. You
wouldn't believe what you can get up to if you have the
money.

President Just keep your eye out for any dissent.

Finance Careful, Anton.

President Don't be so prissy, Stepana. We're not making
our investigations public – just having a little sniff
around.

Justice Which reminds me – are you coming rabbit-
hunting this weekend?

President Not now, Ammos! My head is too full of this
'undercover' agent. I'm just waiting for the door to burst
open and . . .

The door bursts open. Enter Robchinski and Dobchinski, out of breath.

Robchinski You won't Adam and Eve it!

Dobchinski Seriously you won't!

All What's happened?

Robchinski It stretches the bounds of credibility.

Dobchinski Unbelievable!

Robchinski Impossible!

Pause.

All What!

Robchinski Wel . . . there we were . . .

Dobchinski . . . at the Marriott . . .

Robchinski (*interrupting*) Dobchinski and I had just ordered our coffees . . .

Dobchinski (*interrupting*) Please, Peter, let me tell it my way.

Robchinski But you'll put the wrong spin on it.

Dobchinski But you'll miss things out.

Robchinski I won't miss anything out. Just shut it for a second, don't interrupt! Mr President, please tell Peter not to interrupt me.

President Just spit it out, will you! I'm about to have a heart attack!

Robchinski (*to Dobchinski*) I'll do it. I'll do it! (*to the President*) I had just left you, Mr President, to go and do a number on the national security speech, just after you'd received that email – well, I was haring it down the corridor . . . Stop interrupting, Peter! The President wants to hear it from me! I sprinted over to Savchuk's office, but he wasn't there. I called Dimitrenko – no luck. I was just texting Stepan Karpov when who should come pelting down the corridor? Peter Dobchinski. So I said to him, 'Have you heard the news about the email?' And he had – he'd overheard your PA. Who had been gossiping with Ivan Kurkov by the photocopier.

Dobchinski She fancies him rotten, tells him everything.

Robchinski Peter, do not interrupt! Dobchinski and I immediately head off to brainstorm the speech. Peter suggests the Marriott. We've just walked through the revolving doors into the foyer when whom should we see sitting in the coffee shop . . . but a young man . . .

Dobchinski Good-looking, in a decent suit . . .

Robchinski Good-looking, in a decent suit, reading *The Times* newspaper, calm as you like, and with a real 'I'm thinking deep thoughts' way about him. I had a sudden itchy feeling and I turned to Peter. 'There's something going on here.' Peter had already caught the eye of the head waiter. They're old mates.

Dobchinski I wangled him the job at the hotel when he came out of prison on that fraud charge . . .

Robchinski (*interrupts*) Peter, please! So Peter whispers to him: 'Who is that man?' And the waiter replies: 'That,' he says . . . Peter stop butting in! You're not the one telling the story. You're totally unqualified to do so. You have a lisp. 'That guy,' he says, 'is an Englishman who has recently flown in on his way back to London and goes by the name of Martin Remington Gammon. He's been here for two weeks already, hasn't left the hotel, sticks everything on the bill, and hasn't paid a cent.' Well, it immediately dawned on me. 'Aha!' I said to Peter.

Dobchinski Actually I was the one who said 'Aha!'

Robchinski You said it first, and then I also said it. 'Aha!' Yes, it's clear as day. He must be the official.

President What official?

Robchinski The official your cousin warned you about. The UN Inspector .

President What are you saying, man? (*Beat.*) Oh God, oh dear God, not him!?

Dobchinski He's on undisclosed business. He's got a flight booked back to London. Who else could it be?

Robchinski It's him, I'll lay money on it. Eyes in the back of the head he has. He noticed everything – the cinnamon on Peter's latte – you know Peter can't have chocolate because of his allergy.

Dobchinski He even took a butcher's at our teaspoons. I was petrified!

President God have mercy on us! What kind of room is he in?

Dobchinski He started in the luxury suite – the one we gave to the head of the IMF commission when they came to negotiate the loan?

Robchinski But three days ago he downsized to the smallest room in the place. Keeping it low-profile.

President And he's been here . . .

Robchinski Two weeks and counting.

President Two weeks! In the last two weeks we've had street protests about the elections, the 'disappearance' of that wretched journalist woman, and a complete breakdown in the city's sanitary operations. It's bedlam out there! It's a pigsty!

Education Anton, do you think we should all go and present ourselves at the Marriott?

President Brilliant idea, Luka. Why don't we all parade outside his room with signs hung round our necks saying 'Guilty As Sin'?! No, I need to find a way to get to him without him suspecting. He's English, you say?

Dobchinski To his boots.

President Just my luck! The unimpeachable English! Why isn't he Italian? We mustn't let him know we know. As far as we're concerned he's an ordinary businessman. We'll need to show him something. Georgy, the hospital – when are they shooting the 'blind girl under the bus' episode?

Health Today. In trying to save her legs they also miraculously restore her sight.

President Perfect. If we whizz him through the sets quick enough he'll never notice the difference. Get over there now. Explain the situation to them, say the President needs them to put on the performance of their lives. Stepana, we need to show him a road heading North.

Finance I could get some 'North' signs made in English.

President Do it. Stick them on the dual carriageway heading out to the ski slopes. And Ammos, empty the prison of everyone except the politicos. Rapists, murderers, homosexuals, let them all out. Then go to the new IKEA store and buy three hundred and fifty Solveig sofas, they're affordable but stylish. Put one in each cell with a nice tungsten lamp. Bright colours. And put in books. Lots of books. Dostoevsky, Tolstoy, Chaucer! Shakespeare! You there!

Policeman Sir!

President Call your superior officer. I need a limo with exceptionally tinted windows so he can't see how filthy the streets are.

Policeman Sir!

Exit Policeman.

President Let's get going, gentlemen, there's not a moment to waste!

Justice How will I get three hundred sofas through those iron gates?

President Get flat-pack futons. Self-assembly is good for them.

Exeunt all except President, almost bumping into the Policeman, who is returning with the President's terrifying Head of Security, Svistunov, who never smiles.

Ah, Svistunov, there you are. Is the motorcade ready?

Svistunov Ready, sir. The windows are so dark you'd swear it was a moonless night.

President I want bodyguards. Six should do, just to give me a bit of welly. And contact those students – the ones we hire for pro-government rallies. Put them on every bridge to wave as we pass. Dobchinski and Robchinski, you can help me decide what to say in the car. (*to Svistunov*) And tell the militia: no shooting at gypsies today. Let's go, Dobchinski. And remember – he's an ordinary businessman. Let's go! (*instantly returning*) Christ, I forgot. That journalist who disappeared, the one investigating corruption . . .

Svistunov Lizaveta Korshnik.

President Where is she?

Svistunov She's still in your personal interrogation centre.

President And?

Svistunov We're encouraging her to consider an alternative career. She takes a little persuading.

President Well, keep her in until he's gone. And make sure that damned tongue of hers stays silent! It could destroy us all! If he asks about her, we'll say she's gone on holiday. To the Philippines.

Everyone exits. The First Lady, Anna, and her daughter Maria run in. Maria in a tight top and jeans.

Anna Where are they, where are they? (*throwing open the door*) Anton? Darling? Anton! (*to Maria*) This is all your fault. All that fussing – 'Oh my hair, oh my lip gloss.' (*Calls on her phone.*) Anton! Where are you going? Is he here? What do you mean, who? The inspector of course? What's he like? . . . What do you mean, later? Typical. 'Later, later.' At least tell me what country he's from! I said . . . (*with disgust*) He's gone! He'll pay for this. And as for you – taking half an hour to choose the tightest T-shirt in existence. We've missed the whole drama because of your obsession with showing your tits to that Dobchinski. You think he fancies you when actually he retches whenever you turn your back.

Maria Don't be gross, Mum. We'll know everything soon enough.

Anna Oh terrific. We'll know 'soon enough', will we? That kind of attitude is exactly why this country is currently one hundred and fourth in the world league. Why, when the President of Azerbaijan gets to dine at the White House, Anton and I are given ten minutes and a mug of tea with a deputy at the State Department! This guy can change all that! I want to know who he is!

What country is he from? Does he share my love of culture? But no, thanks to you, we have to wait like silly Communist women. Just stand here at this window and wait.

Which is exactly what they do . . .

Act Two

Sammy lies in a small double bed in a room in the Marriott Hotel.

Sammy Christ I'm hungry. I am utterly famished. It's like the Iraq war is taking place in my stomach. We'll never get back to England at this rate. If he didn't insist on lording it in every city we get to . . . He takes cabs everywhere, flies first class, stays only in Marriotts and Intercontinentals, eats in five-star bistros, and then wonders why we don't have enough money to fly home. Martin Gammon. The worst estate agent ever. Worked for Foxtons but got sacked for overenthusiasm and underachievement. He set up on his own, out of a third-floor office in Balham High Street above a haulage company trafficking Serbian whores. Gammon Associates, luxury sales and lettings. The plurals are misleading. I was his only associate and we only ever sold one flat. One particularly uneventful afternoon, he looks up from his paper. 'Sammy, our fortunes lie in the East.' He's been reading about some public-school crook making millions snapping up property in the ex-Soviet Union. Next day he cons his dad into giving him a few grand, adds a stupid middle name to make him sound posher, and hops on a plane. For some unfathomable reason I tag along. We've started six property businesses up to now. All have gone belly up inside a month, we've been beaten by hoodlums throughout most of the Caucasus, and now we find ourselves in a country so miserable even the rats are leaving. It's been a roaring success. Ah, London! Safe, warm, snug little London. In London you can go to the greyhounds one night and the opera the next. You can go to movies and concerts, eat in cosy little restaurants, eye up French students on the tube. You can go boating in Hyde Park and in the next boat will be a celebrity chef, or a lifestyle guru, or a supermodel. You can pop into Harvey Nick's and browse. You can pretend you're married and get the gorgeous-smelling women to put a bit of spray on your wrist, so you can just stand there gulping in the aroma of their skin and peeking down their cleavage. Ah, London! Red Routemasters, black cabs who always know where you want to go, little pastries from Italian delis, peanut-sellers by the Thames, the chimes of Big Ben, the curries of Bethnal Green. Ah, London! The quiet alleyways of the old city on a Sunday, the cobbles clacking beneath your feet, the whiff of bagels from a Jewish bakery, the peal of old Bow bells, oranges and lemons, the bells of Saint – let me take you by the hand and lead you through the streets of fucking wonderful London! And now I'm in Shittskyberg. What am I going to do about him? His old man's refused to send us any more money. And now the hotel management's on our case about our extended stay. Won't give us any more credit in the restaurants until we've settled the balance. What happens if we can't find the money? Oh, for a teaspoon of cabbage soup! I could eat the whole world. What's that stomping? Sounds like our man.

He hastily jumps off the bed as Gammon enters. He wears a classy but faded suit, worn too long.

Gammon Take these. (*Gives him an umbrella and his coat.*) You've been rolling on my bed again.

Sammy I haven't touched it!

Gammon You liar, you were rolling. I can see your arse imprint.

Sammy What would I want with your bed? I've got my own, haven't I? Oh no, I forgot we had to give it up, so now I'm sleeping on the floor in here.

Gammon I need fags. See if there are any in that drawer.

Sammy Dream on. You finished the last one a week ago.

Gammon Tea?

Sammy We drunk all the Milkmaid packets last night. They refused to replace them. And it gets worse. They've taken the porn off our telly.

Gammon They've what?

Sammy No more babushkas with big boobies.

Gammon Impossible!

He tries the telly.

They've scrambled the image! I can't see a thing! That's censorship! Totalitarians! (*He peers at the TV.*) Is that a vagina?

Sammy I think it's an owl.

Gammon Christ, this is dismal. (*He ruminates, then speaks loudly, decisively.*) Pay attention, Samuel!

Sammy Oh God, what now?

Gammon (*less decisively*) Pop down . . .

Sammy Pop down where?

Gammon (*not decisive at all, almost pleading*) Downstairs . . . to the restaurant . . . Tell them . . . to bring me a bite to eat.

Sammy No way. I'm not going down there. They might put me in a lorry and take me away.

Gammon You ungrateful slob! After all I've done for you, nurturing your career . . .

Sammy What career? Anyway, what's the point? The management's refusing to serve us.

Gammon Call yourself a friend!

Sammy They're threatening to go to the authorities. (*Puts on Russian accent.*) 'This is third week you two not pay for anything. You are English rogues, your young friend is piece of shit and you are nasty scum.'

Gammon You're loving this, aren't you? Sadist.

Sammy It's what they said. 'Your friend is crook who comes over here, spends money he is not having, and is thinking we cannot do anything. But don't be kidding yourself. We can go right to the top, and have you put behind bars.'

Gammon That's enough! Just go and get me some food!

Sammy Can't I just phone them?

Gammon First rule of business. Always use the personal touch. (*Pleads.*) Go on. Go on.

Sammy All right. But this is the last time.

Gammon I love you. I really really love you. (*imperious*) Well, get a move on!

Sammy leaves.

It's inhuman how hungry I am. I've been practising mind control. 'I am getting less hungry, I am getting less . . .' No, it's just as bad. I shouldn't have let rip in Tblisi with all those gorgeous Georgians. That painter could play a mean game of poker. I was only with him for half an hour and he skinned me of everything. What would I give for another go at him? Or at his wife. I don't know if I'm hungrier or hornier. The women around here! The foyer downstairs is like one enormous Bond girl audition. But they're only interested in money. You could be one of those dwarves from *Lord of the Rings* and they'd shag you if your wallet was fat enough. But me – I'm invisible.

Six months in the Eastern bloc and not one conquest. What a dump this country is! An apology of a nation. I can't even get credit at the greengrocer's. (*Whistles an aria by Prokofiev, then a song by Britney Spears, then nothing in particular.*)

Enter Sammy and a Waiter. The Waiter speaks with a slight accent.

Waiter You called, sir.

Gammon Ah yes, my dear good friend. How are you, are you well?

Waiter Yes thank you, sir.

Gammon And the hotel – everything running smoothly?

Waiter Everything's fine thank you, sir.

Gammon Plenty of passing trade?

Waiter Enough to be going on with.

Gammon Good, I'm so pleased. Oh, by the way, they haven't brought my meal up yet, could you hurry them along? I have an engagement after lunch.

Waiter Yes, sir, the management has asked me to tell you that you are not to receive any more food. They are looking into it with the authorities.

Gammon Into what exactly? I'll completely waste away at this rate. This is no joke, I am seriously ravenous.

Waiter Yes, sir. The management is of the opinion that you are not to receive another meal until you pay up.

Gammon Well, go and make them see reason.

Waiter What should I say, sir?

Gammon Just drive home the point that I must eat. Maybe you lot can go a day without eating, but you've had three hundred years of practice! I'm from the West. I need filling up three times a day!

Waiter I will talk to him, sir.

Exit Waiter.

Gammon It's pure native meanness, that's all it is. I've never felt this hollow. What can I sell? My trousers? I can't go back to London without trousers. I have to make an impression on my return. I wonder if Barry Fields still has that Bentley. He could pick me up from Heathrow. I'd get Sammy to open the door for me. That would turn a few heads! I'd go straight to the Ivy, step out of the Bentley just as some film producer's going up the steps with the latest starlet. One of the hostesses comes out and smiles prettily. 'Good evening, my name is Martin Remington Gammon. Property magnate. I believe you have a table for me.' On my way in I see a young actress dining alone. I sashay over to her. 'Excuse me, but I couldn't help noticing . . .' Christ, I feel sick I'm so hungry!

Enter Sammy.

Gammon Yes?

Sammy They're bringing lunch.

Gammon Ah haa! They're bringing lunch! They're bringing lunch! They're bringing lunch!

Enter Waiter with the food.

Waiter The management wish to stress that this is the very last time.

Gammon Oh the management, the management . . . The management can eat my shit! What have you brought me?

Waiter Soup and roast beef, sir.

Gammon Two courses? Is that all?

Waiter Yes, sir.

Gammon But that's absurd! I demand an explanation!

Waiter The management say there's plenty there.

Gammon But look at it. Where's the gravy?

Waiter There isn't any gravy, sir.

Gammon Well, I can see that! I can see that for myself, thank you very much.

Waiter I mean there isn't any gravy today, sir.

Gammon Liar! I saw some myself, when I was passing the kitchen, there was oceans of the stuff! And just this morning in the Palace Restaurant two Japanese men were dining on salmon, rocket salad and loads more besides.

Waiter Well, there is some and there isn't some.

Gammon What is that supposed to mean?

Waiter The salmon is on the international menu. That's for the international guests. You've got what the staff and the locals can afford, sir.

Gammon You really are a prick, aren't you?

Waiter Yes, sir.

Gammon You're a peculiarly nasty little specimen. These Japs – why can they eat and I can't? I want quiches, I want swathes of escalope and red mullet. What's so special about these 'international' guests?

Waiter They pay, sir.

Gammon I'm not arguing with you, you moron. The staff! The locals! (*He tries the soup.*) Do you seriously call this soup? You've just poured water into the bowl.

It doesn't taste of anything. I don't want this soup, get me another one.

Waiter I'll take it away, sir. The management say if you don't want it you don't have to have it.

Gammon (*guarding his food with his hand*) Well, listen, I mean to say . . . Oh, just leave it, you cretin! Is this how you always treat people? Well, let me tell you something, I am not of that element. You're clearly not used to dealing with people of my . . . (*Eats.*) Christ, this soup is hideous! Has anyone in the world eaten such hideous soup? There are feathers swimming around in it. (*Holds up a piece of chicken on his fork.*) Call that chicken? No no no, I'll try the roast beef. Sammy, I've left a spoonful of soup for you, tuck in. (*Slices the roast beef.*) What kind of beef is this? This isn't beef.

Waiter What's wrong with it?

Gammon God alone knows what it is, but it isn't beef. It's carpet from the restaurant, roast carpet, that's what it is. (*Eats.*) Swindlers, what are they feeding me! Eating one mouthful gives you lockjaw. (*Picks his teeth.*) Vermin! It's like eating a tree. I can't get the bark out of my teeth. Cheating swine! (*Wipes his mouth with a napkin.*) Is there any more?

Waiter No.

Gammon Thieves! Criminals! You could have given me a bit of gravy. Or some pie. Idle filth! Go on, get out! I'll write to Mr Marriott about this! Fleecing innocent wayfarers, I don't know.

> *Sammy has licked the soup bowl clean. He and the waiter clear the plates and exeunt.*

Seriously though, I am still utterly starving. I could murder a cream bun from the market. Oh, for some bloody money!

Sammy (*entering*) I don't know how to put this, but the President of the country is here to see you.

Beat.

Gammon The President? Of the whole country?

Sammy I told you the management have friends in high places. He's been downstairs in the foyer making enquiries.

Gammon Where is he now?

Sammy In the corridor. With some officers.

Gammon Officers? What kind of officers?

Sammy The unbelievably frightening kind.

Beat.

Gammon Well, go on then, throw me in prison! Just you try it! You'll soon see the kind of man you're dealing with! (*Beat.*) Sammy, is there a fire exit handy? (*He runs to the door and peeks round briefly before closing it fast.*) He's right outside! Did you see what was in their belts? No! No! I don't want to go! I don't want to! I know what their prisons are like! Filled with cockroaches and bad poets. The President himself, eh? That seems a bit draconian. I mean, who does he think he is, just wandering in here! How dare he! I'm not some common Joe, some run-of-the-mill tourist. (*Draws himself up to his full height.*) I'll tell him to his face. 'How dare you, how dare . . .'

The door begins to open. Gammon shrinks in fear, going very pale.

The President enters, followed by Robchinski. Sammy salutes. Gammon hides behind the bed. The President can't find him and is terrified. When the President and anyone else from the country speaks to Gammon or

Sammy (i.e., in English) they speak with an Eastern European or Russian accent, but revert to no accent in the asides and when talking to each other (i.e., in their own language). During the scene Dobchinski peers in from time to time.

Robchinski Please where is Martin Remington Gammon?

Gammon Who wants to know?

Robchinski The President of the country is here to speak with him.

Gammon peeks over the bed. The President leaps in shock. They stare at each other goggle-eyed with fear.

President (*recovering slightly*) Your good health, sir.

Gammon And yours.

President I apologise for the intrusion, but a highly unusual situation has occurred.

Gammon It's not that unusual! I mean, talk about an overreaction, it's only a couple of grand! No one's died, for Christ's sake!

President (*aside*) Why is he talking about money and death? What does he know?

Robchinski (*aside*) Just press on, sir.

President You have been specially selected for a presidential tour . . . out of the thousands of ordinary businessmen who visit this hotel . . . we have chosen you. Please come with us!

Gammon No . . . no way! . . . I know where you're taking me!

President Please . . .

Robchinski Please . . .

Gammon (*stammering at first, but growing in volume towards the end of the speech*) Look, what do you want me to do? I'll pay up . . . my father's posting a cheque even as we speak . . . That waiter! He's the guilty one! That beef he gave me was like reinforced plastic! And the soup! Christ – I shudder to think what he put in it. Starving me to death all day . . . The tea stank of fish. So why should I? I ask you. Why should I?

President Please assure yourself I knew nothing of this. I personally always buy the best beef available. Please, if anything is not to your liking . . . maybe we could move you to a more comfortable room . . .

Gammon No, I don't want to! I know your game. A different room eh? You mean a prison cell! How dare you? What right do you have? I mean to say . . . I am a servant of Her Majesty and the British government! I . . . I . . . I . . .

President (*aside to Robchinski*) He's furious! Our opponents must have already got to him! How could we have been so lax!

Gammon (*to Sammy*) What are they saying?

Sammy Don't ask me. I failed French CSE.

Gammon Don't talk in gobbledegook to me! I know what you're up to! Well, go on then! Call in those thugs you've got outside, they'll have to drag me out! If one of those animals so much as touches me, I'll take this straight to the Ambassador! Who are you? What do you want?

President (*trembling all over*) Please let's talk about this! I've worked all my life. I have a wife and children. I'm sure we can come to an arrangement.

Gammon No, I won't go! And what's that got to do with me? Just because you've got a wife and kids, I'm supposed to be stuffed into some rat-infested cell! Terrific! No, my kindest regards to your prison cell, but no thank you.

President (*still trembling*) Put it down to inexperience. I'm not used to dealing with such large sums of money. Maybe I did receive the odd – how do you say? – favour but such pitiful amounts. A new standard lamp here. A little something for the mantelpiece. And as for that journalist who was investigating this 'financial corruption', I swear no violence has been done to her and it was nothing to do with me. Last thing I heard she was back-packing in Manila.

Gammon What do I care about Manila? (*thinking now*) And why do you keep banging on about this journalist and violence? . . . You wouldn't dare try anything physical with me, would you? Christ I know these countries are barbarous but there are limits. I'll pay, okay? I'll pay! It's just right now there are cashflow issues.

President (*aside to Robchinski*) A likely story! How do I make my move?

Robchinski Be brave, Mr President! Take the bull by the horns!

President Yes, of course! How?

Robchinski Offer him money.

President Brilliant! (*to Gammon*) If it's money you need, or anything else, come to think of it, I am at your service. It is my privilege to assist our foreign guests . . .

Gammon Go on then! Lend me some money! I'll settle with the manager right now. A couple of grand should do it.

President (*taking out envelope*) I happen to have some dollars . . . two thousand exactly. You needn't count them.

34

Gammon (*taking the money*) Well, thank you. Thank you very much.

Sammy Now that's what I call a result.

President (*aside to Robchinski*) He took it!

Robchinski (*aside to the President*) There you are, sir. It'll be plain sailing from now on.

President (*aside to Robchinski*) I gave him five thousand just to be sure.

Robchinski (*aside to the President*) That's the mark of a great man.

Gammon The old man's wiring the money to me any time now and I'll give it straight back to you. Sammy, go and find that pesky waiter. Get him up here.

Sammy exits.

(*to President and Robchinski*) Well now, I'm seeing a very different side to you. But please, gentlemen, take a seat. I beg of you.

President Oh no, please, we prefer to stand.

Gammon No, I insist you take a seat. Now that I appreciate the honesty and goodness of your intentions . . . I confess . . . (*He laughs.*) I thought you'd come here to put me in . . . (*He laughs, they laugh.*) To send me to . . . (*to Robchinski*) Do have a seat. I would offer you tea but we're clean out of Milkmaids.

They sit.

President (*aside to Robchinski*) We must stay on our guard. He obviously wants to remain undercover. Well, two can play at that game. (*aloud*) I was just taking one of my presidential walkabouts with my aide here, I like to keep me in touch with the people, when I think to myself,

'I must check up on how our international guests are being treated.' It's partly duty, partly a Christian love of mankind. I walk in here and I say to the management, 'I want to meet an ordinary international businessman.' They chose your name completely at random from their computer.

Gammon And just as well. If you hadn't come, I think I would have been stuck here for ever. I had absolutely no idea how to pay! (*They all laugh.*)

President (*aside, to Robchinski*) Oh, he's laying it on thick!

Robchinski (*aside, to President*) No idea how to pay!

President (*aside, to Robchinski*) Ha! (*aloud*) And where are you heading after your stay here?

Gammon Straight back to London.

President (*aside, to Robchinski*) He says it as if it meant nothing. He's a class act! (*aloud*) So, this is the end of your travels?

Gammon Afraid so. I thought I could make a mint out here exploiting the new economies. Everyone said there were opportunities for dodgy property agents, evading planning regs, developing green-field sites and so on – but you've got it taped, it seems to me. The whole thing's been a bit of a damp squib really.

President (*aside, to Robchinski*) God, he's good. Trying to draw me into revealing my hand with his tales of corruption. (*aloud*) And are you staying much longer?

Gammon Not if I can help it. Problem is, to get here I borrowed a few grand off the old man, but it's all gone and the bastard won't send me any more. I've got to get back to London. It's the life I'm used to. I can't be doing with this kind of place.

President (*aside, to Robchinski*) He's UN all over. On the surface completely ineffective. But watch out! One slip and he'll tear you apart. (*aloud*) What you say is so true. This is a thankless country. Take me – I am slaving day and night with neither perk nor reward. I don't complain but I don't expect I will ever be recompensed. Unless of course in Heaven. (*Casts his eyes upwards, and then over the room.*) This room is a bit small, in my view.

Gammon It's minuscule. And utterly anonymous. I could be anywhere in the world.

President And it's a little dark, too.

Gammon Pitch-black is what it is. You need to get those peasants to pedal faster!

He laughs, they laugh.

I can't read, can't jot down any of my thoughts.

President I was just thinking . . . Dare I . . .? But no, I'm not worthy.

Gammon No, go on.

President No, I am not worthy. I am not worthy.

Gammon Are you all right? Spit it out, man.

President Dare I . . .? I have a rather beautiful room in my residence that you could . . . No, no, you are just an ordinary businessman, I don't want to put pressure on you to accept such unbelievable luxury . . . Only please don't be angry at my spontaneous act of generosity. I'm a simple man.

Gammon On the contrary, I would be delighted.

President You would make me so happy! And my wife will be overjoyed! That is the kind of man I am. Even as a child I loved to give, in particular to a higher class of person. And don't think I'm saying all this to flatter you.

Never! I am incapable of flattery. Is it my Slavic blood? I have to speak from the depth of my soul.

Gammon I am the same. Is it my true-blue English blood? I can't abide hypocrites. There's nothing I value more in a man than integrity and respect.

The Waiter enters, followed by Sammy.

Waiter You called, sir?

Gammon Yes, peasant, get me the bill.

Waiter I've only just given you a bill, sir.

Gammon Well, I can't remember every damned bill you've brought here. How much do I owe?

Waiter Well, there's the room. And then there's everything that's gone on the room.

Gammon Just tell me how much I owe!

President Please, let us not concern ourselves with that now.

Robchinski (*to Waiter*) Piss off or you'll live to regret it.

Waiter I'll piss off.

Robchinski Good decision.

Waiter exits. As he does, Dobchinski pops his head round. He gets the thumbs-up from Robchinski and enters.

President (*to Gammon*) Someone will take care of that later.

Gammon Quite so, you're quite right. Well, this is more like it. (*He puts away the money.*)

President I wondered it I might propose a tour of the city. In particular its more recent developments in line with the International Monetary Fund's proposals.

Gammon What exactly is there to see?

President Oh well, you can for example see how much progress has been made . . . modernising . . . liberalising . . . privatising . . . I thought you might be interested?

Gammon Why not? Let's go.

President We could start at the prison. Look at some of the Swedish methods we are implementing.

Gammon Really?

President Then there are the schools. You can see how the teaching has embraced the Washington consensus.

He laughs at his joke. Gammon laughs loudly.

And then you must see the new hospital, IMF-funded, of course. (*disingenuously*) I don't suppose you know much about it?

Gammon Nothing, no.

President Of course not. Ha ha. But it's really worth seeing isn't it, Robchinski?

Robchinski A triumph of global capitalism.

President I happen to have a limousine downstairs, or would you prefer to go, how do you say, 'under your own steam'?

Gammon No, the limo sounds good.

President (*to Dobchinski, quietly*) Listen, when we've gone call Georgy at the hospital. Tell him to prepare a spread in the TV crew's canteen. Lots of meats and Madeira. Then go back to my wife and give her this. (*to Gammon*) May I be so bold as to borrow some paper? I want to write a list for my wife.

Gammon Oh, all right. You can use this bill – I won't be needing it.

President Thanking you so much. (*writing and aside*) And we'll see what a healthy dose of plum brandy can achieve. Doesn't look like much but it can knock over an elephant.

He finishes the note, gives it to Dobchinski.

Let's be on our way. Your . . . colleague can take your luggage on to the residence. (*to Sammy*) There'll be a car outside. Ask for the Presidential Palace. Dobchinski will accompany you. (*He turns to Gammon.*) Please, after you, sir, after you.

President, Robchinski and Gammon leave. Dobchinski remains. Sammy picks up a pair of pants from the floor and puts them in a suitcase. Then a vest. Then a mouldy toothbrush. Pause.

Dobchinski Please, take your time, sir.

Sammy No, I think that's pretty much the sum of it. Shall we to the palace?

Act Three

The same room as Act One. Anna Andreyevna and Maria Antonovna are still standing exactly as at the end of Act One.

Anna We've been standing here an hour now. All because of your fussing. We've spoiled you, that's the problem. When I was your age I spent two hours a night washing the coal from my father's back. You spend it gazing at your own arse.

Maria (*opening the window to get some air*) Just chill out. We'll know everything soon.

Anna But where the hell is everyone? It's like they all died.

Maria (*looks out of the window and screeches*) Mum, look! Look! A government car's coming up to the gates!

Anna Where?

Maria There! There's someone getting out. There!

Anna You're imagining it, you fantasist!

Maria Buy some glasses and you'll see.

Anna I don't need glasses! There's no one there! Oh yes, so there is. Who is it? He's wearing a suit. Christ, this is driving me crazy! Who could it be?

Maria It's Dobchinski.

Anna What do you mean, it's Dobchinski?! There you go again with your insane fantasies.

Maria For God's sake, Mum, it's Dobchinski.

Anna You're just picking a fight for the sake of it. For the seventh time, it is not Dobchinski!

Maria Then who is it? Who? Look. It's . . .

Anna Yes, it's Dobchinski all right. Why are you making such a big deal of it? Who's the nasty little fat man walking next to him? (*She shouts out of the window.*) Dobchinski! Why are you dawdling? Where are they? Just shout it from there man, it doesn't matter. (*Steps away from the window.*) Little twerp won't say anything until he gets inside.

 Enter Dobchinski, completely breathless.

Well, go on then! Speak!

Dobchinski I got here as fast I could. Good afternoon, Maria. You look very nice.

Maria Whatever.

Anna Come on, spill the beans, man.

Dobchinski I have a letter from your husband.

Anna Yes yes yes, but is he the UN official?

Dobchinski The very same. Peter Robchinski and I were the first to know.

Anna Well, go on then. Who? What? When?

Dobchinski Well, basically, I think we're in the clear. He was pretty tough with the President at first. He got mighty worked up about the way he'd been treated at the hotel, and refused our offer to come here. Then when he realised it wasn't the President's fault, and they'd had a bit of a chat, he changed completely, and after that it all went smoothly. They should be at the hospital by now . . . Have you seen *Ambulance Division*?

Anna Oh yes, I love it. It's so realistic.

Dobchinski Well, here's hoping. There was a moment when we thought he'd already sent New York his report. I was so scared!

Anna Oh, grow up. What's he like? How old is he?

Dobchinski Late twenties, maybe. But he speaks with a maturity beyond his years. (*Speaks with accent, i.e. in English.*) 'I've got to get back to London . . .' The guy oozes class. 'I adore to read and write,' he says, 'but in this light . . .'

Anna Is he dark or fair?

Dobchinski He's sort of in-between. And he has such quick eyes, like a ferret. It freaked me out.

Anna You're such a wimp. I've always loathed you. What does my husband have to say for himself? (*She reads.*) 'Darling Anna, just a quick note to tell you that for a while I was consumed in despair, but two club sandwiches with extra fries, three plates of luxury beluga caviar . . .' The man's insane. Club sandwiches and caviar?

Dobchinski Oh sorry, I forgot, he wrote the note on a hotel bill.

Anna Oh I see. 'But I think all will now be well. Prepare a room for a VIP. Make sure there is lots of wine and nibbles for the reception, and brandy, the strongest we've got. My darling, I kiss your hand and remain for ever yours.' Oh my God, he's coming. Who's out there? Michka!

Dobchinski Michka! Michka! Michka!

Enter Michka, a young house servant.

Anna Listen. Run down to the cellar and grab twenty bottles of red. Use the stuff given us by the French foreign minister, that should be half-decent. And see if you can find some plum brandy.

Maria There's some in the boot of my Audi. I ran out of antifreeze.

Anna Order the string quartet. Get the red carpet out of the cupboard. And prepare the yellow room for a guest. VIP treatment.

Dobchinski Anna Andreyevna, I might just pop over to the hospital – see how it's going.

Anna Well, go on then, no one's stopping you!

Dobchinski Goodbye, Maria.

Maria As if.

Exeunt Dobchinski and Michka in opposite directions.

Anna We must get ourselves ready, Maria. UN. Understated but fashionable. You should wear the ice-blue Versace.

Maria No way! It's so last-year. Now all the middle classes are wearing it and it just looks plain! I'll wear the D and G Daddy got from Moscow.

Anna You'll look much better in the ice-blue. It will complement my yellow perfectly.

Maria But yellow doesn't suit you.

Anna Doesn't suit me!

Maria Your eyes aren't dark enough.

Anna Are you implying I don't have dark eyes? They're positively nocturnal.

Maria And it makes you look fat.

Anna Oh bullshit. How little you know about colour!

They go out. Servants pour in preparing the reception. Wine. Canapés, including oysters. Michka enters with a red carpet and with old bedclothes, Sammy through the other door with cases. Michka puts down the red carpet. He speaks English in a thick accent.

Sammy Oy, you there. Where am I taking this?

Michka Are you with the VIP?

Sammy Uh, yes. Yes, that's me.

Michka In there, please, old man.

Sammy Old man? Cheeky bugger. How far is it? A man can't walk on an empty stomach.

Michka Pleasing you, old man, will your Secretary-General be here soon?

Sammy My who?

Michka Your general?

Sammy I don't have a general.

Michka points to the bags.

Michka He is not general? I thought . . .

Sammy Well . . . I mean to say, he is and he isn't. He's not that type of general.

Michka Is that more like real general, or less?

Beat.

Sammy More.

Michka (*whistles, impressed*) So that is why everyone here is getting hot under their collars!

Sammy Listen, you appear to be a bright sort of a lad, get me something to eat, would you?

Michka Please. You must wait for VIP food. You will not like the food we servants eat. It is, how you say, very bog-standard.

Sammy Well now. What sort of bog-standard would that be?

Michka Just some soups, some hams, some salamis, some cabbages, some meat pies . . .

Sammy Yup, that'll do. Go, bring me soup, salami and pies! You can skip the cabbage. Am I going this way?

They go out in different directions, through side doors.

A fanfare. The chandelier lights up. String quartet enters hurriedly. The big double doors are thrown open. Gammon enters, accompanied by the President, the Ministers for Education, Health, Finance and Justice. Down the red carpet. A sudden impression of grandeur. Posed photographs. Camera flashes. Bodyguards. All the paraphernalia of an official function. Tables are brought out, canapés brought in, the plum brandy poured out and the wine decanted.

Gammon That was really fascinating, some wonderful places. I'm impressed by the way you show visitors around. It hasn't happened to me anywhere else.

President If I may be so bold, that's because the governments of other countries in the region are more concerned with pursuing their own interests. But here we realise the value of the ordinary businessman. And why? Because you are the future. You represent a freer and better world for all of us.

Gammon belches.

Gammon That brunch was gorgeous. Do you have that every day?

President It was especially laid on for our distinguished guest.

Gammon I love eating. That's what life's about, to my mind: plucking the flowers of pleasure. What was that fish we had?

Health A labardan, sir.

President A national delicacy – very rare.

Gammon Bit like haddock. And where was that we ate?

Health In the hospital canteen, sir.

Gammon Yes, I remember, there were some beds. Well, may I congratulate the hospital on the quality of its food. No wonder all the patients look so perky. I've never seen such knockout nurses either. Wonderful legs.

Health Thank you, sir.

Gammon And the way they all burst into tears having brought that blind girl back to life. There they were operating on her pelvis and her eyes opened!

President To think the very first thing she saw on God's earth was your face.

Health No wonder she was so happy.

Gammon She was a bit of all right, too. No chance of meeting up with her again, I suppose? I just felt we clicked in our brief time together.

Health We mustn't interrupt the healing process.

Gammon I was hoping to contribute towards it. Where were all the other patients? I only saw six in all.

Health That's because the hospital is very well managed. The minute I was appointed Minister, the patients started recovering like flies. These days people have scarcely arrived at hospital before they're cured and back out again.

Wine, brandy and canapés are being passed around on trays.

President Yes, but if I may be so bold, all this is part of a bigger master plan which as President I oversee, in co-ordination with the international bodies. Do take a glass of wine. The loan from the International Monetary Fund has conditions which a lesser man would find onerous. Social programmes, such as the improvement of prisoner conditions which you witnessed.

Gammon Hmm yes. Lovely pink futons.

President The new roads to the North . . .

Gammon What wonderful big signs you have.

President Of course we're dealing with hundreds of millions of dollars here. A lesser man might take advantage of my position, to seek to benefit personally at the expense of society as a whole. Do try some sushi. For me if the streets are clean, the hospitals empty, the prisons like hotels, and political unrest at an all-time low, that's reward enough. Have a sausage. No financial remuneration, honours, Nobel Prizes – they are flattering of course, but compared with a virtuous act, what are they but dust and vanity?

Gammon What you say is very true. I myself like to meditate upon the world from time to time. I sometimes put it down in writing, scribble a spot of prose, or dash off the lyrics of a song. This wine is very drinkable.

His glass is refilled again.

Tell me, is there anything to do in this city? Maybe a club where I could play cards while semi-naked women dance around poles?

48

Everyone laughs.

President (*aside to Health*) Sharp as a knife! But we know what he's getting at! (*to Gammon*) God no, sir! We've made every effort to drive the gambling mafias right out of the city. I myself have never picked up a card in my life. And as for women, that sort of industry gets no look-in here!

Lots of shaking of male heads.

Education (*aside to Justice*) Just last night he took half my wallet off me at the Lusty Lagoon!

Enter Anna and Maria, all togged up.

President Come in, my dear. May I be so bold as to introduce my family to you. My wife and daughter. Mr Gammon is a property investor.

Gammon (*finishing another glass of wine and bowing deeply*) Madam, I am blessed that in my lifetime I should be granted the pleasure of meeting you.

Anna Oh, but it's much more of a pleasure for us to meet a man of such distinction.

Gammon I am forced to disagree with you, madam. The pleasure is all mine.

Anna You're just saying that to flatter me! I beg you, do sit down.

Gammon It is enough to stand in your presence. However, if you insist. (*He sits.*) There. My happiness is complete.

Anna I don't know whether to take your compliments seriously. I would have thought that, after London or New York, coming here would be rather tiresome for you.

Gammon Incredibly tiresome. One is accustomed, don't you know, to moving within the higher echelons of society.

49

(*He moves on to the brandy, takes a swig, gasps.*) So of course to find oneself on the road – (*Swigs.*) – in the moribund desolation of international hotels – (*Swigs again.*) – brushing sleeves with the common tourist and, heaven help us, the native population – well, I'll be candid. Present company excepted . . .

Anna It must be awful for you.

Gammon *Au contraire, madame*, at this moment it is extremely agreeable.

Anna (*flushing terribly*) You can't be serious, sir! I don't deserve such sweet words.

Gammon Why don't you deserve it? Madam, you deserve it.

Anna But our country is so small, so backward.

> *Gammon is emptying the many glasses of red wine and brandy laid out on the trays and reception tables.*

Gammon But it has its charms. The simple honesty of its people. Their amusing attempts at the latest fashion. Of course it can't be compared to London. Now that's a city! You're probably aware by now I'm no ordinary estate agent.

President Well, far be it from me to say . . .

Gammon Well, you're right, my friends. I am on speaking terms with the managing director of Bovis Homes. We go for beers together in O'Neill's. Sometimes I email him and straight away in my inbox there'll be a funny reply or an invitation to play five-a-side. Come and play five-a-side, Gammon. I can't tonight. Oh, go on. No, really. Don't be such a flannel, Gammon! No, I really can't . . . Go on! Oh, all right then, twist my arm. He wanted to get me involved on the planning applications side at Bovis. We're talking six figures. But I've always hunted alone. But ladies, gentlemen, please, why are you standing? Do sit down.

Justice No, let us stand for a bit longer, we know the protocol.

Education I love standing. It's my favourite position.

Gammon Oh, bollocks to all that cod formality, have a seat! There you go. Park your arse on that.

Everyone sits.

I can't stand ceremony. Quite the opposite. I try to go about my business without being noticed. Only it's not so easy, I can tell you!

Everyone laughs.

I only have to take a walk down Balham High Street and it's, 'Ah, Martin Remington Gammon as I live and breathe!'

Anna It must be awful for you.

Gammon It's the price you pay for being a legend.

Anna You must be terribly influential. In government circles.

Gammon I'm quite a mover/shaker. I have my own think-tank. The Gammon quango.

Anna Oh yes, I've heard of it.

Gammon Yes, I write the manifestos for all the major parties.

Anna You don't say.

Gammon They're always publishing my views in the newspapers. I have a property column in *The Times*. A political column in *The Guardian*. And a gossip column in the *Mail*. I know all the TV actresses and the A-list celebs. I'm constantly dining with playwrights. I was on *Big Brother* with Pinter. I said to him, 'Pinter, you old bastard, how are you?' 'So-so,' he says. He's a character.

Anna So you're a writer too?

Gammon In my spare time. The National has two plays on at the moment. And as for novels – *Enduring Love*, *Our Mutual Friend* and *The Mill on the Floss* are all mine. That was just an accident really. I didn't want to be a writer, but all the movie moguls were on their knees: 'You've got to write a screenplay.' So I thought, 'Well, if I must.' I wrote *Notting Hill*, *Speed 2* and *Chariots of Fire* in one weekend. Have you heard of Wilbur Smith?

Anna You're Wilbur Smith?

Gammon Yup. And I help a lot of writers. Penguin employ me as a shadow writer on romances to up the erotic ante.

Anna I'm guessing, but is *White Teeth* yours?

Gammon Spot on.

Anna I knew it!

Maria I thought that was written by Zadie Smith.

Gammon No, she's right. That one is written by her, but I wrote another one.

Anna I think I read yours. It's very funny.

Gammon I adore literature. I own the biggest house in Hampstead. If ever you're passing, just drop by. My parties are notorious. (*He drinks some more wine.*)

Anna They must be the height of magnificence!

Gammon You don't know the half, man. I have all fresh and wild exotic fruits along one table. Watermelon, mango, pavaya, guapa. All hand-picked by free-to-wander

Fijians. I have oysters from France even when there isn't an 'r' in the month. Champagne on tap. And I get the best bands in to play. Dire Straits. Norah Jones. That was a charity gig in aid of the Asian tzatziki. They all came to that. The Minister, the Prime Minister, the General Secretary, the Secretary-General.

All stand timidly from their chairs.

I attend all the big functions. I'm not just in *Who's Who* I'm in *Who's Who's Who*. One Wednesday I was put in charge of the whole Clapham branch of Foxton's. My boss suddenly upped and left. Childcare crisis. Well, pretty quickly questions were being asked. Who's going to take charge? There were viewings in the diary, keys to be collected. Who could cope with the pressure? Well, the Lord Chancellor tried. So did the Chancellor of the Exchequer. But they couldn't take the heat. Oh, it looks easy, but when it's five twenty-nine and someone wants to know whether a property's Streatham Hill or Brixton borders, that's the test of a man! So in the end they turn to me. 'Martin Remington, please come and take over the Clapham branch! Spare us from chaos!' I wanted to turn it down, but I thought to myself, Her Majesty will hear about this, and there's the New Year's honours list to think about. So I say, 'I'll take the job, but I tell you what, I'm going to run that branch of Foxton's like a devil! I won't bend the rules. I won't offer favours. I won't stand for gazumping!' Pretty soon word got round. Gammon's in charge of Foxton's! Wakey-wakey! Smell the coffee! Men from the boys! Wheat from the sheep! No more Mr Nice Guy! Every time I walked across the office floor it was like an earthquake erupting in their hearts! They were shaking like leaves!

Everyone shakes with fear. Gammon is getting more and more excited.

So they should! I make no apologies. I can't stand deception! That's the kind of man I am! You hide those cracks in the walls – I'll find them! You paint over the rot – I'll expose it! I AM EVERYWHERE. I SEE EVERYTHING. I'm at the White House every month, we pray together in the Rose Garden and watch baseball and eat pretzels in the Oval Office. He's planning on making me Secretary of State for the Defensive Interior of Homeland Security . . . (*He slips and almost falls sprawling on to the floor.*)

President (*shaking all over, tries to speak*) Y-y-y-your . . .

Gammon (*abruptly in a sharp voice*) What do you want?

President Uh. Y-y-your . . .

Gammon Speak up, man, you're talking gibberish.

President Y-y-y-your Leniency, Your Expediency . . .

Gammon Get off me. What? You want to take it outside? You want to? Come on then, I'll take you on. I'll take you all on!

President Won't you have a lie down? We have a room for you, with everything you'll need.

Gammon What crap! Why would I want a lie-down? Actually maybe I will have a lie-down. You know what – that brunch was really . . . Thanking you most kindly, thank you most . . . (*Shouts.*) Labardan! Labardan!

He goes into the side room, followed by the President and several servants. Beat.

Robchinski That is one serious player.

Justice What is Foxton's?

Dobchinski It must be a club used by the Security Council.

Education Oh God.

54

Health Luka, calm down!

Education Oh God! Oh God!

Health Luka, get a grip! So what if he is a member of the UN top table? So what if he dines personally with Kofi Annan! You seriously think the IMF are going to stop the flow of capital for that bunch of poofs? They don't give a toss what we're doing in the privacy of our own home as long as we're paying the bills!

Education But what will happen when he compiles his report? They'll find out about everything – the Swiss school-fees account, the oil pipe in my garden, the disappearing poll booths . . . Yelena will divorce me! My father will deny me to my face! Oh, why did we ever leave Mother Russia?

Finance Gentlemen, there are ladies present. May I suggest we discuss our options in private?

Justice Stepana's quite right. This is not for a woman's ears.

Finance Good afternoon, Madam President.

Education Good afternoon, Anna Andreyevna.

Dobchinski Good afternoon, Maria.

They exit.

Anna What an incredible man he is! Why do we have no one like him?

Maria He's so gorgeous.

Anna His manners! His eye for fashion! You could see he took a shine to me. Couldn't take his eyes off me.

Maria He was looking at me!

Anna Oh, put a sock in it. No, really, do shut up.

Maria Get real, Mum!

Anna Why on earth would he be looking at you?

Maria He couldn't stop looking at me. When he was talking about exotic fruits he glanced at me, and when he talked about Nora Jones he looked at me again.

Anna Well, he may have let slip a glance in your direction. He probably thought, 'Poor thing, I should at least try and look at her once.'

Enter the President, looking deathly pale.

Anton, is something wrong?

President I took him into the VIP room. He was standing on the yellow bed pretending to be a fish. Like this. Then he collapsed onto the sheets. I thought he was asleep. I started to look through his pockets.

Anna Anton, you . . .

President I just wanted to know who he is! All these people visiting us, checking up on us. G8, NATO, EU, WTO. The same suits. The same Palm Pilots. Who are they all? Suddenly I felt an icy hand on mine and there he was, staring deeply into my eyes. He looked at me with a deathly smile and whispered: 'Internal viewing highly recommended.' Then he laughed like a madman!

Anna What does it mean?

President It means he wants to see the North! He knows. He knows! He's toying with me like a snake with its prey! I can feel his coils round my neck. Tightening. Tightening.

Enter Sammy, eating the remains of a pie.

Anna Who is that repulsive little man?

President Shhhh! It's his bodyguard.

Anna He doesn't look like a bodyguard.

President I know, brilliant isn't it? (*to Sammy*) Is he sleeping?

Sammy Not yet. He's having a little stretch.

Anna What's your name?

Sammy Sammy, madam.

Anna I'm Anna, but you can call me Madam President.

President (*to his wife and daughter*) Will you get out of the way! (*to Sammy*) Come here, my friend, don't be shy. So how long have you been working for your boss?

Sammy He's not technically my . . .

President You know what, Sammy? I like your face. I think you and I could really hit it off. I'm really taking a shine to you. (*Punches him playfully.*) You're my sort of guy. (*Punches him again.*) I've got something for you. I'm sure it's not normal procedure to accept gifts but maybe you can declare it . . . or maybe not . . .

He winks and gives him some money. Sammy takes it.

Sammy Thank you very much.

President Not at all . . . good. So then, my friend . . . the role your boss plays in the 'organisation'. I imagine it involves meeting a lot of international leaders?

Pause.

Sammy Yes. International leaders do sometimes pop round.

President What rank is he in the 'organisation'?

Sammy Oh the . . . usual sort of rank. High. Top rank.

President Just as I thought.

Maria Does he have a girlfriend?

Anna What kind of women does he like?

President Will you stop harassing him! Focus on the main issue! (*to Sammy*) And what's your role in relation to him? I'm guessing you're looking after his security?

Sammy Security, yes.

President I knew it! Go on, what are you? MI6? CIA? You can tell me.

Sammy I can't.

President Oh, please go on!

Sammy No, really, I can't. No, I really can't.

President What a pro! I bet no one messes with Sammy! (*Punches him playfully again.*)

Sammy They certainly don't! (*Punches him playfully back.*)

President What kind of a man is he? Is he really the type to be blowing the whistle on people for a little indiscretion here or there?

Sammy He's absolutely the type. You won't find a tougher customer anywhere in the 'organisation'.

Maria What kind of figure does he like best?

Anna I'm sure what excites him is a woman's mind.

President Will you both belt up? (*to Sammy*) So – what's the focus of the current trip? Economic stewardship? Electoral issues? Human rights abuses?

Sammy Abuse – that's a big focus.

President Really?

Sammy Oh yeah. Some of the places we visit, he asks me, 'Sammy, how did they treat you?' 'Badly, boss.' 'Sammy,' he'll say, 'these people are poor hosts. Remind me of this abuse when I come to compile my report.' Of course I'm just a simple person.

President I've already given you a little something, haven't I? But maybe you need a little more? Life's so expensive these days.

He hands him some more money.

Sammy Very generous of you, sir.

The President holds on to the money.

President And in return maybe you could see fit to dissuade your boss from any 'internal viewings'. Maybe raise a few security concerns?

Sammy Yes, I reckon I could do that.

President Good lad.

He hands him some more money. They laugh. Enter Svistunov.

Svistunov Mr President, may I have a private word with you?

President Can't it wait until later? Oh all right. (*to the women*) You two – out of here. Shhh! Don't make a sound.

Exeunt Anna and Maria.

(*to Sammy*) Well, my dear friend, please go to your boss. And remember – internal viewings!

Sammy exits. President turns to Svistunov.

I want twenty armed men at the gate and another twenty at the rear. Word's bound to get out that he's here. I don't want any of the scum getting near him. Particularly not opposition parties, foreign journalists or anyone with a petition. If you so much as catch a glimpse of someone trying to get through those gates, grab the little bastard and dispose of him. (*loud*) Dispose of him, you understand me?

Svistunov Yes, Mr President.

President Shhhh, don't shout, man! Can't you hear he's sleeping? Christ, you KGB types are such thugs! Well, go on then! What was it you wanted?

Svistunov It's about Lizaveta Korshnik.

President Who?

Svistunov The journalist we took in for questioning?

President Oh yes – The bitch hasn't got out, has she? Christ, she could cause chaos with what she knows!

Svistunov No, sir.

President What does that mean?

Svistunov You asked me to ensure her tongue didn't blab. My men took your instructions to heart.

President What do you mean?

Svistunov produces a human tongue. The President freezes in horror, holding his heart. Gammon's deep snores can be heard from next door.

Interval.

Act Four

The same room. A few hours later. The Ministers of Health, Justice, Finance and Education and the Head of Intelligence all creep into the room followed closely by Dobchinski and Robchinski.

Justice Get in here immediately, all of you! Can we please have an orderly line? This is a man who spends whole afternoons shaking hands on Capitol Hill!

Health What's the point of going through the motions at a time like this?

Justice The President requires our assistance. We have to do something!

Education How is he?

Robchinski The seizure sent his heart rate to three times its normal level.

Dobchinski He's off the chart.

Justice Is he sedated?

Robchinski The doctors tried, but he kept escaping.

Dobchinski They've locked the doors to the East Wing.

Justice It's down to us, gentlemen.

Intelligence So what's the plan?

Justice The plan? Well, I thought . . . to start with . . . we'd just say hello.

Health Ammos, due to the overenthusiasm of our security service a female journalist no longer has a budding radio career! The bastard is this close to getting the story! You think mass handshaking can help us now?

Finance I know what would.

She has taken a small vial from her handbag.

Health Stepana, what is that?

Finance It's from my KGB days. I carry it in my handbag in case of emergencies.

Education What are you suggesting?

Finance I saw some syringes in the President's bathroom. Svistunov could find the appropriate artery . . .

Health Stepana, for God's sake! He's an international figurehead. We can't just bump him off.

Finance Heart attack in his sleep. Happens all the time.

Health And then what? They'll send someone else to investigate. Probably a whole team. Are you going to murder them too? How much serum have you got?

Finance Well, what's your big idea?

Health We need to slip him a bribe and get him out of here. A cool hundred grand when no one's looking. It worked with that economist from Washington.

Justice But he was a businessman. He understood the way of the world. This guy's an idealist.

Health Then make it five hundred grand. Call it a donation to the UN Humanitarian Fund.

Intelligence I could say my operatives found a suitcase of money on the street with his name on it.

Health I'll throw you on the street in a minute. Someone just needs to go in there, sweet-talk him round and give him the money. You do it, Ammos.

Justice Why don't you do it? You've already had brunch with him.

Health (*getting out of it*) On second thoughts I think Luka should do it.

Education Why me?

Health You represent the hopes and fears of our children.

Education (*getting out of it*) No, I can't! It's my upbringing. I lose it completely when I'm talking to someone more important than me. And my English is dreadful! Please don't make me!

Intelligence I'll do it.

All No!

Health Okay, we'll all do it. One by one. Ammos, you go first.

Justice Why me?

Health When you speak it's like listening to Nelson Mandela . . .

Justice Just because I get carried away talking about my beagles . . .

Health No, it's not just dogs, you once spoke very movingly about the human genome.

All (*pestering him*) Go on, Ammos, please, Ammos . . .

Justice Oh, just leave me alone!

Intelligence By the way, what should I do with this?

He is holding up the tongue.

Finance What the hell is that?

Intelligence It's the journalist's tongue.

Health What's it doing in here?

Intelligence Svistunov gave it to me to dispose of. I am his superior, you know. I wasn't sure if I should give it back to the family.

Health Hide it! Put it away!

Intelligence Where?

Sudden coughing from Gammon's room. The Head of Intelligence stuffs the tongue in his pocket. Everyone runs to the other door, in mad terror, crushing themselves in the mêlée to get out.

Robchinski Owww! Peter, you trod on my toes!

Education Help! I'm being crushed to death!

And a few more exclamations before they all squeeze out of the door.

Enter Gammon, sleepy-eyed.

Gammon What a lovely snooze. Nothing like a real feather mattress. I didn't half sweat, though. I think they might have slipped something into that brunch. I certainly didn't drink that much. I could really see myself settling in here. I do love it when people are gracious with their hospitality – such genuine shows of affection, quite unstained by personal ambition. It's humbling. And the daughter's eminently shaggable. You can see her nipples through her dress. Yes, I could get used to this.

Enter Justice Minister, surreptitiously clutching an envelope.

Justice (*to himself*) Oh God! Oh God! Help! My knees are giving way under me! (*drawing himself up, to Gammon*) May I have the honour of introducing myself. I am Ammos Fyodorovich Lyapkin. Minister of Justice and Interior Security.

Gammon Please take a seat. Minister of Justice, eh?

Justice Yes, I was given the post when the President was elected after the 1991 revolution. (*aside*) I don't know where to sit! It's like walking on burning coals!

Gammon And you're still in the same position fourteen years later?

Justice Yes, we're very fortunate that the people have freely chosen the same government in four elections since. Just last year, in a resounding endorsement, ninety-five per cent of the electorate voted for the party. (*aside*) Why can't I sit? Sit, man. Sit! (*He does not sit.*)

Gammon The opposition can't have been very happy.

Justice They took defeat most ungraciously. Made all sorts of wild unsubstantiated claims. (*aside*) Oh, this is torture!

Gammon What's that in your hand?

Justice (*confused, drops the envelope*) Oh, nothing.

Gammon What do you mean, nothing? You just dropped that envelope.

Justice Me, sir? I don't think so. (*aside*) Oh God, I'll be arrested on the spot. I can already see the tribunal at the Hague.

Gammon opens the envelope, which is stuffed full of money.

Gammon This envelope is stuffed full of money.

Justice (*aside*) That's it. I'm done for!

Gammon Listen, I've had an idea. Can you lend me this?

Justice (*in a rush*) What, sir? I mean how, sir? I mean yes, of course, sir! (*aside*) Pull yourself together! I am strong! I am strong!

Gammon It's a funny thing but I've somehow managed to blow all my cash on this trip. Of course I'll send it to you once I'm back in London.

Justice Oh please, Your Honour, whenever is convenient! I have always done my utmost to serve authority. To use what little power I have . . . to serve! (*Stands to attention.*) I won't presume to disturb you for any longer. Any other demands you wish to make? I would be only too happy to oblige.

Gammon What demands would I make of you?

Justice Oh, I don't know . . . about the justice system for example?

Gammon Why would I do that?

Justice (*bows deeply and exits. Aside*) We're in!

Gammon (*once he has gone*) What a good bloke.

Enter Education, trembling. He speaks English very badly.

Education May I have the honey . . . I am Luka Lukich Khlopov. Minister of Education.

Gammon Come in, come in! Have a seat. Cigar?

Education (*aside*) Oh God! No one told me about this. To take or not to take?

Gammon Go on, take it, it's a decent Havana. They were in a box in my room. I'm impressed you have them in these parts. Of course in London you can get cigars that cost five hundred quid a puff. Here's a light. Smoke away.

Education tries to smoke and gets the shakes.

Try the other end.

Education (*jumps in terror, breaks the cigar, spits, gesticulates wildly. Aside*) Oh damn it! Why am I such a coward? I'm ruined!

Gammon You're clearly not a cigar man. It's a weakness of mine, I'm afraid to say. That and the fairer sex. Now on that subject I cannot remain indifferent. How about you? Which do you go for? Blondes or brunettes?

Education is quite unable to reply.

Come on, you can tell me. Blondes or brunettes?

Education I – I– I am not wishing to be expressing an onion, sir.

Gammon Oh come on! You must have a penchant one way or the other.

Education Well, if may take the library – (*aside*) I haven't a clue what I'm talking about!

Gammon Ahhh! I see! You don't want to tell me. But I can guess. Someone recently had an encounter with a pretty brunette? Go on, am I right? Am I?

Education is silent.

He's blushing! You did! You did! Why not just admit it?

Education I don't have the courgette, Your Apostrophe –

Gammon I don't blame you for being coy. It's my eyes. They instil fear in the hardiest of men. And in women they instil something quite different. Am I right?

Education Oh yes, sir.

Gammon You know, a funny thing happened to me on my travels here. I blew all my money. You couldn't lend me five thousand dollars?

Education (*aside*) Where's that damned envelope? Oh, trust me to lose it! Oh, here it is. Thank God. Thank God. (*He gives it over, shaking.*)

Gammon Much obliged.

Education I won't depress you any longer.

Gammon Bye now.

Education (*aside as he runs off*) Thank God it's over! And he never even asked about the schools in the North!

Gammon He's also a good egg. I like these people.

Enter the Head of Intelligence.

Intelligence Good afternoon.

Gammon Oh good, someone else. And you are?

Intelligence I am the President's Head of Intelligence.

Gammon Come in. Come in. I was just thinking how much I like this country. Of course it's not in the major league, am I right?

Intelligence You are right.

Gammon You only really meet top quality in the West. We're light years ahead of you emerging provinces when it comes down to it. Wouldn't you say?

Intelligence I would absolutely.

Gammon But can a man really be happy in a parochial backwater like this?

Intelligence Oh yes, absolutely.

Gammon Yes, I suppose so. I mean what do we need to be happy? To be liked. Liked and respected. (*Beat.*) Anyway, that's what I think.

Intelligence I absolutely agree.

Gammon Do you? Really? People in England think I'm a bit odd. It's just how I am. (*Beat.*) Something quite bizarre occurred to me on my travels. I blew all my money. You couldn't lend me ten thousand dollars?

Intelligence Why on earth not? I just so happen to have on me . . . (*He reaches into his pocket to take out the envelope, but picks the wrong pocket and takes out the tongue instead.*)

Gammon What's that?

Intelligence This? This is a tongue.

Gammon Do you always carry tongues around with you?

Intelligence Yes, quite often.

Gammon May I? (*He takes it.*)

Gammon It must be some kind of joke tongue. (*He waggles the tongue.*) Rather realistic. (*to Intelligence*) Mind if I keep it?

Intelligence No no.

Gammon Very generous of you. I love practical jokes. Now I think you were about to give me a lot of money?

Intelligence (*takes out an envelope*) Yes, sir. Here, sir.

Gammon I'm ever so grateful. I hate denying myself goodies when I'm travelling. And why should I? Don't you agree?

Intelligence Absolutely, sir. May I go now, please?

Gammon Of course.

The Head of Intelligence exits. The sound of a frantic conversation.

Enter Health with his official briefcase, smoking and looking very pale.

Health May I have the honour of introducing myself? Minister of Health Georgy Zemlyanika.

Gammon Hello.

Health I'm sure you're far too busy to remember, but I showed you around the hospital this morning?

Gammon Oh yes, that's right! What a terrific brunch you dished up.

Health I aim to serve the international community in whatever way I can.

Gammon I remember you as being a little shorter, am I right?

Health It's quite possible.

Minister of Health takes a glance at Gammon. Gammon looks at Minister for Health. In the scene other Ministers – Education, Intelligence, Justice, Finance – may begin to poke their heads round the doors, hide in corners etc.

Gammon Can I help you?

Health I was just wondering . . . I think you may have chanced upon an unfortunate item.

Gammon I don't think so. Oh, you mean this? (*He holds up the tongue. Pause.*)

Health Yes.

Gammon Yes, rather funny, isn't it? I wonder whose it is. (*He waggles it.*)

Health Okay, let's stop playing games.

Gammon I couldn't agree more!

Health sits.

Pause.

Health They're listening to our conversation so I have to be very careful what I say. I want you to know that since

70

my appointment I have been unstinting in my application to freedom, democracy and the global market. (*Moves his chair closer.*) But I wish that were true of everyone. What you have in your hand is only scratching the surface. The Minister for Education sends his kids to private schools paid for by foreign charities. The Minister of Justice is an unreconstructed Communist who beats people up for voting against us. The Head of Intelligence operates surveillance on all newspapers and imprisons anyone who writes a word against the regime. The Finance Minister has siphoned off millions from the various privatisations. They've stripped the assets of most of our industry and laundered the profits into foreign accounts. I tell you this only out of love for my country. These men are my dearest friends and comrades, but can you see how I cannot condone their behaviour?

Gammon Can I see? Well, yes . . .

Health No, sir, it's time for change. Were I . . . were I for example to be given a leading role . . . Or indeed, if I may be so bold, were I to be granted a presidential role in a new administration – supported by the American government and the United Nations – I can say to you categorically that un-American activities like this would not be tolerated! No, sir. Not tolerated! Use what you have in your hand. Include what I've told you in your report, the stink you will cause will give me the platform I need to challenge the President. At which time I am confident I will receive the full support of the State Department in Washington and all that goes with it. I have received positive indications in private meetings with US operatives active in the city, and money is already waiting in several offshore accounts to bankroll my campaign. We both want rid of this guy. Now's the time to make it happen.

Pause.

Would it be better if I wrote some of this down for you?

Gammon Yes, I think that might be better. I love reading stories when I'm bored. I've completely forgotten your name.

Health Zemlyanika. It means strawberry.

Gammon Oh yes, that's right. Now I remember.

Health I won't take up any more of your valuable time. Look after that. (*the tongue*) It will bring us all liberty.

Gammon Really? (*Shouts.*) Hey, you! What's your name again? I've forgotten it.

Health (*poking his head round the door*) Georgy Zemlyanika. It means strawberry.

Gammon Listen, Strawberry, a funny thing happened to me on my travels here. You don't have fifteen thousand dollars on you?

Health I have a lot more than that.

He opens his briefcase. It is packed with dollar notes.

Gammon Blimey, that's a bit of luck.

Health To liberty and the free market.

Health exits. Gammon looks at the tongue, shrugs, and then pockets it.

Dobchinski and Robchinski enter.

Robchinski Allow me the honour of introducing myself!

Dobchinski Allow me the honour of introducing myself!

Gammon uses the tongue as a puppet and replies.

Gammon Allow me the honour of introducing myself!

Dobchinski/Robchinski Aaaagh!

Gammon Don't worry, it's only pretend. Good, isn't it?

They all laugh.

Dobchinski/Robchinski Very good, sir. Very good.

Gammon I know one of you but I can't remember which. (*suddenly and abruptly*) Got any dosh?

Dobchinski Dosh, sir?

Gammon Lolly. Green. Money.

Robchinski What kind of money?

Gammon Ten thousand dollars?

Robchinski Well, sir, not on me, I mean to say . . . (*to Dobchinski*) look in your pockets, Peter, quickly . . .

Dobchinski I don't think I carry that kind of cash . . .

Robchinski Maybe in the lining of your jacket? You know how it falls through.

Dobchinski Nothing has fallen through.

Gammon Oh dear.

Robchinski Well, hold on, that needn't be an obstacle. Maybe, if you were to be so kind as to give us your account details, we could set up a little account for you in Belize or Zurich.

Gammon Can you do that?

Dobchinski Oh yes, we've done it for all the ministers.

Robchinski And even for one of our IMF friends. My brother's in an organisation that specialises in that sort of thing. 'It's easy when you know how.'

They laugh. Dobchinski is setting up a laptop and printing out a form.

Robchinski How much would you like for starters? Fifty thousand? Sixty?

Gammon That sounds reasonable.

Robchinski Just sign here. We'll have that set up by the end of the day. And it can be topped up whenever you need.

Gammon Excellent.

Pause.

What?

Dobchinski Your Excellency . . .

Gammon Yes, what is it?

Dobchinski The . . .?

Gammon Oh this? What about it?

Dobchinski Well, we . . . I thought we . . . Didn't we, Peter?

Robchinski We were wondering if maybe we could . . . have it back.

Gammon Oh no. I want to show it to my friends back in London.

Pause.

Robchinski But I thought we had an agreement.

Gammon I don't think so.

Robchinski We get the tongue. You get a little gift.

Gammon News to me.

Robchinski No, it's not news to you.

Dobchinski Calm down, Peter.

Gammon Yeah, cool it, would you? It's only a bloody tongue.

Robchinski No, I will not cool it. You take me for a ride, I'll take you for one – off the White Cliffs of fucking Dover!

Dobchinski Peter.

Robchinski I have cousins in London. You want to meet them?

Dobchinski Peter, shut up!

Robchinski You want an umbrella spike in the leg on Waterloo Bridge? I've done it before! You want that? You want it?

Gammon Well, I'm definitely not giving it to you now. You've got no sense of humour, you lot.

Pause. Dobchinski laughs. All the Ministers (except the Finance Minister) come from their hiding places and laugh. Robchinski laughs.

Oh, I see! Oh, good one! Good one! You had me there! God, you devils! Come on then! Come and get it. Come and get it.

Enter the Finance Minister.

Finance You have state property in your possession. Give it to me.

Gammon (*laughing*) Is this still part of the joke? No, maybe not.

Finance grabs his arm.

All right, no need to get pushy. Oy, get off!

Finance grabs the tongue. A small tussle, at the end of which she stuffs it in her mouth and eats it. Pause.

Well, that wasn't very clever, was it? I was going to have fun with that, you killjoy! (*Beat.*) Are you all right?

Finance Fine. I won't take up much of your time.

She glares at the others, who leave. She hands him a package.

Gammon What is this?

Finance It's a gift from the Russian government. They knew I'd be seeing you.

Gammon opens it. It's a gold bar.

There'll be more if you stop this country from pursuing its ill-considered plans to join NATO.

Gammon Me stop them from . . .

Finance My Russian friends don't want the enemy building any kind of military base in this country.

Gammon The enemy?

Finance The Cold War is over but there are limits to the thaw. We don't want a US pipeline across our northern hills. We don't want a Starbucks on every street. We are proud of our heritage. We are proud to follow in the footsteps of Peter the Great. Leave us alone and no one will come to any harm.

Gammon Do you know, I have absolutely no idea what you're talking about!

He laughs. She laughs. He laughs. She laughs. They both laugh.

Finance I think we understand each other.

Gammon It's been a pleasure.

Finance (*at the door*) Anton is not a bad man. When we were nineteen we used to sit on the lawns of the university making flags for the Vietcong and discussing dialectical materialism. He was a dreamer then. She ruined him. She is the one you should be destroying.

Exit Finance Minister.

Gammon I have a feeling they may have mistaken me for someone else. Maybe I went a bit over the top this morning. I'm going to email Ian Scully in London.

Enter Sammy, eating a cake.

Samuel! Get me a laptop with an internet connection!

Exit Sammy.

Scully can write a funny piece about it – he might even get it in *Private Eye*. If he can be bothered to get off his fat arse, he's actually got quite a tongue on him. This trip has proved quite profitable after all.

Enter Sammy with laptop, which he sets up on the table.

Sammy With the compliments of the President.

Gammon Notice how they treat me here? At last someone's seeing my real worth.

He throws Sammy the money.

Sammy What's this?

Gammon Just some long overdue tokens of appreciation.

He throws Sammy the gold bar. Pause.

Sammy Okay, I'm thinking . . .

Gammon What are you thinking?

Sammy I'm thinking it's time to get the hell out of here.

Gammon (*typing*) Why in God's name would we do that?

Sammy My mother always said: 'Quit while you're ahead.' We've never been ahead so we've not had much practice. At some point they're going to find out you're not who they think you are. And then what? I've noticed a helipad on the roof. We could be out of here in minutes.

Gammon (*typing*) Oh, all right. Go and sort it out. Invent some high-powered reason why we need to go. They can take us to the nearest civilised country and we'll fly home from there. (*still typing*) Scully is going to die laughing when he reads this.

Sammy exits. Gammon continues typing. The light begins to draw in. Dusk. We hear Sammy in the background.

Sammy (*off*) Oy, you. My boss and I require a helicopter to be ready in half an hour, to take us to the nearest civilised country. It's an official visit so we won't be paying. Half an hour or there'll be hell to pay.

Gammon There goes my last chance of Soviet sex. I wonder if his email address is still the blueyonder one.

He presses 'Send'. Sammy returns.

There. Sent.

The sound of voices in the street outside the window.

Voices Let us in. You can't stop us! We want to speak to the UN Inspector! We have a right to speak to him.

We hear the Security speak on megaphones.

Security Clear the area. Move back from the gates.

The noise gets louder, more and more people crying to be let in.

Gammon What's going on out there? Sammy, go and see what the noise is about.

Sammy (*looking between the curtains out of the window*) It's some kind of demo. There's about five hundred people shouting to be let in. The soldiers are keeping them back. The people have got banners and petitions.

Gammon What do they want?

Sammy I think they might want to see you.

Gammon Then who am I to deny them?

Sammy I really don't think that's a good idea.

Gammon I'm sure you're right.

Gammon dodges Sammy, goes to the window, squeezes his head through the curtains. A roar greets his appearance.

What do you want, my good people?

Voices Let us in! We want to speak to you! Tell them to let us in! Let us in!

Gammon Send a delegation and I shall hear it. Let them in, I say! That's an order! Go and open the door, Sammy.

Sammy exits. A petition flies through the window. Gammon picks it up.

'To the representative of the United Nations. We come to you on bended knee as our last hope for freedom in this country . . .'

Gammon pauses. Enter Sammy, with a delegation of small businessmen, all beaten-down and haggard-looking.

Gammon Well, how can I help?

Businessman 1 We come to plead justice!

Gammon Really?

Businessman 2 Save us from ruin, sir! Stop our suffering and the insults heaped upon us.

Gammon By who?

Businessman 1 By the President! When he came to power he promised a new era of freedom. He promised to support small businessmen like us. Now he gives all the contracts to his friends and to foreign companies who he says can do the job cheaper. He says we are not efficient. But we have no roads, no railways, we cannot transport our goods, we cannot compete! And then he raids our offices, claims we are evading tax, just to fill up his own coffers!

Gammon You don't say. The little swindler!

Businessman 2 We have to pay the Mafia for protection from the government and the government for protection from the Mafia. He sends his henchmen in to strip our factories. We have to hide everything. And then he makes up new rules on the spot. Last week he declared his birthday to be a national holiday. Every business in the land has to give him a present! What are we supposed to do?

Gammon The man sounds like a common thief!

Businessman 1 He is, Your Honour. But you try to argue, he shuts you down on some technicality and throws you in jail on a tax-evasion charge.

Gammon He should be hauled up in front of the Court of Human Rights!

Businessman 1 Oh yes, Your Honour, that's exactly what we need. We're willing to fund any action you might need to take . . .

Gammon Oh no I couldn't even consider it. Bribery is anathema to me. However, a small loan to help oil the wheels of change would be quite a different matter.

Businessman 1 Whatever you need. Please take ten thousand.

Businessman 2 Here's five from me.

'Here's ten,' etc., etc. They festoon money on to him.

Businessman 1 And here are just a few examples of the trades and crafts of our country. Please accept them as a sign of our gratitude.

They bring in a tray and a carpet, a scarf and some wine.

Gammon Oh right. Well, yes, I could do with a tray.

Businessman 2 Here is a hand-woven blanket. Please take it.

Gammon Well, why not? Keep me nice and snug on my journey. And the wine. Thank you. (*He is handed a pitiful scarf.*) And this scarf – well, I can use it to keep a door open or something.

Businessman 1 You are doing us a great favour.

Businessman 2 We don't know what would happen if it weren't for you! Please don't let us down! We would hang ourselves!

Gammon Absolutely. Absolutely. The door's just over there. I'll do my utmost!

They go out. The roar from outside is growing. Women's voices are heard: 'Don't you dare touch me! Let me in! Let us in!' Gammon goes to the window.

Who's that down there? Good women, what do you want?

Women Let us in, Your Honour! Hear us! Let us in!

Gammon Very well, let them enter. (*Turns from the window.*) It's turning into quite a gathering. There must be several thousand out there.

Enter two women. They are the journalist's Mother and the Activist.

Mother Your Honour, please listen to me . . .

Activist Listen to us. You have to listen to us.

Gammon All right, calm down, one at a time.

Mother I wish to make a complaint about the President of this country! May he go to the devil! May neither he nor his children ever make profit from this life!

Gammon Yes, but who are you?

Mother I am the mother of Lizaveta Korshnik.

Gammon Who?

Mother She was a journalist, sir, for a city paper, and she came upon evidence, of corruption, his corruption – may he rot in hell, he and his cronies! They've taken the money loaned from the World Bank and put it all in personal accounts in Nigeria and the Congo. My daughter was chasing the story. She had evidence, firm evidence, when one night she disappeared and the evidence went with her. They say they know nothing about where she is. They say she is probably on holiday! Lizaveta does not go on holiday! She is just a journalist, a young woman who asked questions, and now she is locked up in prison, and they won't even tell me where . . .

Enter Svistunov and Security Guards, fast. She turns on them.

Where is she? What have you done with her? I know you know! You all know! (*to Gammon*) I cannot see her! I don't know if she is alive or dead! I have tried Amnesty, I have collected petitions, I have written to British government and American government but no one does anything! He has them all in his pocket! I hope his entire family rot in hell. I hope none of them see God's merciful light!

Gammon But that's appalling!

Mother Please . . . what can you do about it?

Gammon Do . . . well . . . I can declare my sense of outrage and despair, that's what I can do!

Mother And you will bring it up with him. You'll include it in your report?

Gammon Absolutely I will. It's an insult! What about the other one? Who are you?

Activist I'm an activist. I knew Lizaveta Korshnik. We campaigned together for the opposition, such as it is, in the North of the country. Have you been there?

Gammon No, but I've seen the motorways. Wonderful!

Activist There are no motorways! There is nothing! The industries have been closed down to satisfy the loan conditions, and they've just left us to rot. People are dying of illness, children have nothing to eat, nothing to wear against the cold. The electricity has been cut off for three months. They want to kill us because we refuse to vote for the President. And no one knows. The television companies don't dare go there. His nephew owns the main newspaper. Foreign countries pretend nothing is happening so they can get a foothold in our economy. The IMF turns a blind eye. They never come, and when they do, they stay in the best hotels and get taken only to the smart areas. The election was our only chance. I was trying to get the vote out against the President. It was working, there are millions of people in the North and East, we just needed ordinary people to be brave and to go to the polling stations! We had a chance! The military jumped me one night when I was doorstepping. They took me to a warehouse and tried to make me stop my campaign. They stripped me and beat me with electric rods. I have the burns to prove it. But I wouldn't give up. I won't give up whatever they do to me!

Several Security enter the room and begin to drag the women out.

Activist Here they come! But I won't give up. I won't give up! There are more and more of us and we won't be silenced!

Mother We won't be silenced!

Activist We won't be silenced!

As if to echo her shout, the crowd outside roar: 'We won't be silenced.' Holding hands, the women are dragged out. Petitions through the window. Sammy enters and runs over to the window.

Gammon What's all the noise?

Sammy There's a huge crowd developing. They're all waving white flags. Thousands of them! They're getting closer! They're trying to smash down the gates!

More petitions fly through the window. Now hands, dirty, bleeding, through the windows and walls. Pleading, grabbing. Gammon approaches.

Gammon Who's that? Who are you all? (*pushing away petitions*) I don't want it! Get off me! I don't need it! I don't want it! I don't want it!

He retreats from the window.

SAMMY! CLOSE THE FUCKING WINDOW!

Sammy enters and shuts the windows. No more hands through the walls, no more petitions through the window. A sudden quite unnatural silence.

That's better.

Enter Maria in a new tight top.

Maria I didn't know if you were still sleeping.

Gammon Please, no need to be alarmed. Your timing is exquisite. (*to Samuel*) How long have I got?

Samuel Twenty minutes.

Gammon That'll be ample. Goodbye.

Sammy leaves.

As I say, no need to be alarmed.

Maria I'm not alarmed.

Gammon (*striking a pose*) I take it as a compliment that I should have such an effect on a young woman of your charms . . . May I enquire where you were heading?

Maria I wasn't heading anywhere.

Gammon And why weren't you heading anywhere?

Maria I don't need to explain my movements to you.

Gammon That may be so, but I want you to tell me, really, truly, why you weren't heading anywhere.

Maria Why do you speak in such an old-fashioned way?

Gammon I'm an old-fashioned guy. Does it bother you?

Maria No, I like it. In this country, a man's idea of foreplay is parking the Mercedes. That is why I am still a virgin.

Gammon Please grant me the happiness of offering you a chair. Although it's not a chair you deserve but a throne!

Maria You sure know how to talk to a girl. I bet you have lots of practice in London.

Gammon But practice is all it is. I've been waiting all my life for the practice to end. You've changed clothes I see. That top really suits you.

Maria I bought it in Petersburg in my year off. You can't get anything decent in this dump.

Gammon What I would give to be that top, so that I could cling to your lily-white skin.

Maria I bet you have a hundred girlfriends already.

Gammon But none with eyes that tear my soul to pieces.

Maria Are you a poet?

Gammon How did you know? What kind of poetry do you like? I know heaps.

Maria Something romantic?

Gammon Of course, the English romantic tradition. Byron . . . and the other ones like him . . .

Maria Go on then. Tell me some.

Gammon What – now? Okay. How about this? 'I've never seen you looking so lovely as you did tonight. Never seen you shine so bright. You were amazing.' There are loads more. I just can't remember them. But far better that I proclaim my love for you, the love which, as I gaze into your eyes . . .

Maria I don't know what love is. (*Moves away.*)

Gammon (*moves closer*) Why did you move away? It's so much nicer if we're nearer.

Maria (*moves away*) It makes no difference if we're further.

Gammon (*moves closer*) Then it makes no difference if we're nearer. Imagine further is nearer, then nearer will be further. You've lived under communism. You should be used to that kind of logic.

Maria (*disingenuously*) Why should a little provincial millionairess interest a major statesman like you?

Gammon (*moves his chair closer*) But even major statesmen can get lonely. I was lonely sleeping just now. They've given me such a big bed in there.

Maria It's a VIP bed. I used to bounce on it as a child.

Gammon (*kissing her on the shoulder*) I want to see you bounce. On its yellow sheets. Its soft embroidered pillows.

Maria We'll have to be quick. I have a violin lesson at six.

Gammon I adore the violin.

Maria I'm grade seven.

They kiss passionately and make their way towards the door.

Enter Anna.

Anna (*seeing Gammon kissing her*) What the hell's going on?

Gammon Foiled again!

Anna What kind of behaviour do you call this?

Maria What's it got to do with you?

Anna Out of this room! You hear me? And don't you dare show your scrawny little face in here again.

Maria exits.

I'm sorry, sir, but I confess I am rather taken aback . . .

Gammon (*aside*) Now dusk has fallen, she doesn't look bad either. (*Falls to his knees.*) Madam, have mercy on me, I am burning up with love.

Anna What are you doing down there? Get up! The floor is dirty.

Gammon No! I must stay down here, on my knees, and on my knees beseech you to tell me my fate! Life? Or death?

87

Anna Forgive me, but I don't understand. You appear to be declaring love for my daughter, is that right?

Gammon No no no! It's you I'm in love with!

Anna But my dear sir, I am so to speak married.

Gammon Ah, technicalities! True love obeys no rules. But if you cannot tear yourself away from your husband for ever, then at least allow me twenty minutes of paradise – in the VIP room. (*Looks at his watch.*) Make that fifteen minutes.

Anna My dear sir, whatever happened to the English reserve?

Gammon It was made defenceless by your eyes.

Anna No, wait – I need to talk to you.

Gammon Well, can you make it snappy? I have a tight schedule.

Anna Tell me – I value the opinion of a man in your position – do you think Anton can ever really be premier league?

Gammon You mean is he a match for you?

Anna I knew it. He's small fry. I've waited so long for him to move beyond the rabbit-hunting and the aircraft-buying. But it's no good. His idea of happiness is a sun-lounger in the Cayman Islands. But I have dreams. I have a shrewd business brain allied with a skill for diplomacy and a nose for culture. I'm wasting away in this place . . . I'm dying inside!

Gammon This seems to me like perfect pillow talk. Shall we . . .?

Anna I need a man who can match my vision – a man with flair, a man of sophistication and integrity. A man with élan.

Gammon With a what?

Anna I need you, Martin Remington. Take me with you. I have money, I have talent to burn. I can host your parties. I will grace every occasion. I will grace your bed.

Gammon (*joyously*) Result!

Anna You see this oyster? It's the world. And it's ours.

She hurls herself at him and they kiss passionately.

Enter Maria.

Maria Mum, Daddy's escaped from the East Wing . . . (*Sees them and screams.*) Aaah!

Gammon Oh, for Christ's sake!

Maria is crying.

Maria You bitch! You complete bitch! How could you?

Anna What's wrong now? God, you make such a drama of everything! You're like a three-year-old. You would never, ever guess she was eighteen years old. When will you finally grow up? When will you finally behave like a proper, sensible young woman?

Maria (*weeping*) Everything I ever want in the whole world you take away from me!

Anna Oh, get a grip! You're such a provincial fucking airhead, you really are. You're like all the girls in this city.

Maria I hate you! I hate you!

Anna Why do you have to copy all those vacuous floozies? There are other role models. Your own mother stands before you! Had you thought of emulating her?

Sammy enters.

Sammy The helicopter's ready to go.

Gammon What – now? You said twenty minutes! (*He rushes to Maria and clasps her hand.*) Madam President, please do not stand in our way! Give your blessing to our love!

Anna (*in astonishment*) You're not saying . . . it's not her you're . . .

Gammon I want to take her from this hell and fly her to the life she deserves! (*to Maria*) Get your coat.

Sammy (*aside to Gammon*) This is not a good idea. Remember what my mother said.

Gammon (*aside to Sammy*) Your mother hadn't gone six months without a bunk-up.

Anna Will you be mainly in London, or New York?

Gammon Whatever she desires.

Maria I don't know if the Hampstead scene would suit me.

Gammon I'll put it on the market tomorrow.

Anna You could buy a loft apartment in Mayfair.

Gammon I know the one. Three thousand square foot, offering spacious accommodation over two floors, mezzanine gallery, open-plan living space, fully fitted Neff kitchen and private secure parking betwixt leafy Green Park and the fashion mecca of Bond Street. (*to Anna*) And with an adjoining luxury private apartment for selected visitors.

Anna Well, I can see there are advantages all round. You're just lucky I'm not the jealous type.

The President runs in breathless, trailing medical equipment and chased by doctors.

President Your Excellency! Have mercy on me! Have mercy on us all!

Gammon What is it?

President I know what's happened! I've been informed. The people are taking advantage of your presence here! But those idiots out there – they're not the real people. They're criminals, the extremists, the militant element and the lunatic fringe. That woman with the burns on her back is a terrorist! We never touched her. She beat herself!

Gammon I don't give two hoots about her.

President But you mustn't believe them! That stuff about us and the loan money? Lies lies lies!

Anna My dear, you are clearly not aware of the honour Mr Gammon is bestowing on us. He's taking Maria to London.

President What? What? Have you gone out of your mind, woman? Please don't be angry with her, Your Excellency, she's a bit simple, her mother was the same.

Gammon No, it's true. I want to marry her!

President But Your Excellency . . . you must be pulling with my leg!

Anna Look, you moron, read my lips . . .

President I can't believe it!

Gammon Well, all I can say is it's true, and if you do not consent to give me Maria's hand, then God only knows what I am capable of! And when I do shoot myself, it'll be you they come looking for!

President Aaghh no! My God! I'm not guilty! I'm not guilty! Do what you want! Right now my head is . . . Someone tell me what's happening! I feel like a little boy.

Anna Just give them your blessing!

Gammon approaches Maria.

President Well, then God bless you both, but I am not guilty!

Gammon kisses Maria.

Oh my God. (*Rubs his eyes.*) They're kissing. Look, they're really kissing! They're engaged! (*Jumps for joy.*) Oh yes! Yes! Yes! Yes! You God, Anton! You fucking God! What a day it's been!

Gammon Come, my love, we have a chopper to catch.

President You're leaving us already?

Gammon Yes, got to dash. There are some business affairs that need dealing with. All very high-level. I'd say more but it's highly confidential.

President Of course.

Maria We're going house-hunting together. Mayfair . . .

Gammon Muswell Hill . . .

Sammy Merton . . .

President But when will, I mean to say . . . could you give us some idea . . . will there be a wedding?

Gammon (*packing his stuff*) Oh yes, absolutely . . . we won't be long . . . just enough time to put the Hampstead pad on the market, we'll be back at the weekend without fail.

President In that case we won't keep you any longer and we look forward to your safe and speedy return. Just bring her back! (*He laughs.*)

Gammon Absolutely. Safe and speedy. Come, my love . . . Words cannot express . . .

President Do you need anything for the journey? Some money?

Gammon What would I need money for? (*Beat.*) Although on the other hand, yes.

President How much do you think would . . . ?

Gammon Well, this morning you gave me two thousand which turned out to be five. I don't want to take advantage of you. Shall we say another ten?

President (*goes to a safe, takes out money*) Let's bring out some spanking new notes to mark the occasion.

Gammon Oh yes, let's! (*Takes the notes.*) Oh look. World Bank wrappers. Well, goodbye, sir! Or can I say . . . Father? I am deeply indebted to you. I have never in my life been so warmly received. Goodbye, madam. Or should it be *au revoir*? Come, light of my life!

Maria I haven't packed.

Gammon Just bring your eyes. They're the only luggage you'll need.

Sammy This is a bad idea.

Gammon Stop fretting. We'll lose her at baggage reclaim.

He exits. They follow.

Anna Helicopters are chilly things, would you like a rug?

Gammon I have that blanket the businessmen gave me. But I won't say no to another one.

President Someone get one of the fine Persian rugs the Iranian Ambassador gave me. Stick it in the back seat! And bring a hamper of local produce for the journey. Honey, wine, cakes. Bring it all on!

The sound of a helicopter's propeller.

Gammon Goodbye, Anton!

President Please! Call me Tony!

Gammon Cheers, Tony!

President Goodbye, Your Excellency!

Anna (*off*) Goodbye, Martin Remington!

Gammon Goodbye, Mother! Goodbye, dear sweet family!

The helicopter's roar overcomes the stage.

Act Five

Continuation. The President, Anna, return into the room.

President How about that? Did you ever even dream . . .
Go on, be honest, did you ever really dream that you –
a coalminer's daughter – would be related to such a fine
young devil!

Anna Of course I did. It's only you that find this all so
remarkable. You've never known how to mix with the
elite.

President Excuse me, you're looking at the elite right
now. Just think what high-flyers we're going to be! And
screw the rest of them! Hold on, I'd almost forgotten
about those whining bastards outside. Who's there?

Enter Svistunov.

Is that mob still outside the gates? Get some of them in
here, the business delegation that visited our English
friend. I'll teach the little shits to turn me in! I want the
names of everyone who's been out there. Get the CCTV
footage and match it with Ivan's intelligence files. Round
them up and stick them in the prisons, there's space now
we've released the rapists. Find that activist woman who
claims she was beaten – the lying whore – and get rid of
her. I don't want her poking her nose in our affairs again.
Declare the journalist's mother insane and section her. As
for Lizaveta Korshnik, take her scuba-diving. Force the
rest of the crowd to disperse. Use rubber bullets if you
have them, if not the normal kind will have to do. And
tell Dobchinski he can announce the wedding. Call all the
TV stations, I want half an hour devoted exclusively to

the good news. I want the whole fucking country to know by dinner time!

Exit Security.

Well now, my dear. What does the future hold for us? Is it London? Or New York?

Anna We can't stay here, that's for sure.

President As far as the presidency goes, I've had a good fifteen years. And I know Ammos is desperate to have a bash at it. You and I are destined for higher things. How does President of the IMF sound?

Anna I would expect nothing less.

President Imagine the power. Deciding on loans! Who to foreclose on, who to deny. Or would you prefer the UN?

Anna No, the IMF.

President That's my Anna! Always following the money! I'm not fussy. Either way you're in the White House once a month. They'll hold dinners in our honour. Senators and Congressmen will stand around the table waiting for us to sit! What I would bloody well give for that!

Anna God, you're vulgar. Understand that our lives must change completely now. No more rabbit-hunting. No more beer. And no more of that dreadful language you use. It's quite improper in Manhattan society.

President I can't wait to taste the chilli beef and fries with lashings of . . .

Anna All you can think about are beef and fries! I have my mind on higher things. I want one of the finest apartments on the Upper East Side. I want scented candles from Bloomingdales and bath salts from Macey's. (*She sniffs the air.*) Wonderful!

Enter Security, dragging in the Businessmen.

President Ah, here come the vultures!

Businessmen Good evening, Mr President.

President Well now, my little angels, how are we all? How's business? Coming in here to snipe at me behind my back! You scum! Well, I've got news for you, you little shit-stirrers!

Anna Anton darling, there's that language again.

President Who gives a monkeys about language now! Did you know that the very same official whom you came tweeting to is going to marry my daughter. Hmm? What do you say to that, eh? So now it's my turn to chirp . . . I'll . . . ooohh . . . You make up stories about me. You lie to anyone who'll listen, tell them it's my fault your businesses are failing. Look to your own eye! Working three-day weeks, taking the longest lunches known to man, and creaming off the profits at the first opportunity. You're bone idle, that's your problem! I was reared to be tough, school of hard knocks, that's mè, but you! You think it should all be handed to you on a plate! You want feeding? I'll feed you! I'll force-feed you your own shit. I'll shove it right down your own throats!

Anna Watch that heart of yours, dear.

President I'll enter every single one of your offices and if I find a single irregularity I'll send you to the coldest, most miserable corner of this miserable country where you will spend the rest of your days eating nothing but snow!

Businessmen Please have mercy on us, Mr President.

President Yes, they're grovelling now. Why? Because I've come out on top! Well, I forgive you. I'm not a man to bear a grudge. But just you keep a lookout when you're walking down a street alone at night. Just you do that! You haven't even congratulated me! It isn't some district governor she's marrying you know! I have one word to say to you – Foxton's! Ha ha! And don't try and give me some cheese to make up for it! Oh, get out of here. Go on, just fuck off.

They leave. The sound of gunfire from the street and screaming. Then silence. Justice, Finance and Health enter.

Health Anton, if what I hear on the radio is true, Lady Luck has come knocking at your door.

President I don't know if luck's the right word, Georgy, but thank you all the same.

Finance My congratulations, Mr President. Delighted to hear the news. (*She kisses Anna's hand frostily.*) Congratulations, Anna.

Justice Anton, my most sincere congratulations! And you look so well!

President Fully recovered thank you, Ammos.

Justice May you and the happy couple be blessed with a long life, prosperity, with children, grandchildren, great-grandchildren . . .

Enter several aides, officials and politicians who all approach to congratulate.

Official 1 May I have the honour of congratulating . . .

Official 2 I heard it on the radio . . .

Politician Mr President, may I have the honour of congratulating . . .

Official 1 My dear lady, my most heartfelt congratulations.

Official 2 It was on the radio . . .

Enter Dobchinski and Robchinski at the back, jostling for position.

Robchinski May I have the honour of congratulating you, Mr President?

Dobchinski Mr President, may I have the honour . . .?

Robchinski It was on the radio!

Dobchinski On the radio it was.

More shooting from outside. Screams. Dobchinski approaches Anna.

Congratulations, Madam President. Maria is a wonderful girl. As you know, I was hoping I might one day have been so fortunate . . .

Anna Yeah, like that was going to happen.

President Yes, dream on, Dobchinski!

Everyone laughs.

Robchinski Madam President, may I have the honour of congratulating you? London, eh? Tell Maria to wear grungy clothes. And always eat in restaurants with stripped floorboards and no tablecloths. In London poor is the new rich!

More guests invade the room, including the Minister of Education and his wife. More shooting.

Education Mr President, may I just say – you have taken this country to a whole new level!

Wife Anna my darling, many congratulations! (*They kiss.*) I was so pleased when I heard the radio announcement. 'The President's daughter is to marry a top-ranking official in the United Nations!' I almost drove the jeep into the curb! I said to my husband, 'Luka dear, Anna must be over the moon. I'm over the moon,

I must come and congratulate Anna personally. Anna's been desperate for the right match for her daughter and now she's got it!' I was so over the moon I couldn't speak. I cried and cried. Luka said to me, 'Why are you wailing my dear?' 'Oh Luka,' I replied, 'I don't even know the answer to that myself!'

President Ladies and gentlemen, I beg you, take a seat! Bring some more chairs!

The guests begin to sit. The Security enter, including Svistunov. A final rattle of gunfire. Fast and furious.

Svistunov May I have the honour of congratulating you, Mr President?

President Thank you, thank you. What's the situation outside?

Svistunov It's under control, sir. The ambulances are just leaving.

President No television presence, I hope?

Svistunov They're choosing to focus on your daughter's engagement.

President Quite right.

The guests settle. No more gunfire now.

Justice But Anton, do tell us the whole story . . .

President It was extraordinary. He had the good grace to make the proposal himself.

Anna He said it all so beautifully! 'My lady, sweet Anna, my admiration for you and your inestimable qualities . . .' He's so refined, but with a strong moral underpinning . . . 'Believe me,' he said, 'I am doing this purely out of love and respect for you . . .'

President I was a teeny bit scared when he said he would shoot himself if I refused him!

Guests Goodness!

Justice Of all the things to say!

Education Fate is shining on us today!

Health Not fate, old man. This is the reward for true merit. (*aside*) The bastard's got away with it again!

Justice Mr President, you simply must come rabbit-hunting to celebrate.

President No, thank you, Ammos, my rabbit-hunting days are over.

Justice Well, what about pheasants?

Politician And where is the distinguished guest? There was talk he'd had to leave for some reason.

President Yes, he's had to leave on some highly confidential business. He's taken Maria with him!

Whistles of excitement.

She'll be approaching European airspace as we speak!

Anna And with her the hopes of this country!

President But they're coming back at the weekend. (*He sneezes.*)

All Bless you. God bless you! God bless you!

President Thank you. Thanks. But of course at the weekend they'll be back. (*He sneezes again.*)

All Bless you. God bless you! God bless you!

Above the chorus of 'Bless you's we hear the following.

All May God bless you, Mr President!

Robchinski May you live to a hundred and die a rich man, Mr President!

Dobchinski May you live to two hundred and die a billionaire, Mr President!

Health May you die a slow and lingering death!

Wife May you rot in hell!

President Thank you so much. I wish you all the same!

Anna We will of course be relocating to New York in the foreseeable future. The atmosphere here . . . is a little too villagey . . . I confess to finding the whole place intolerable. I'll be starting my own media empire, which will involve regular trips to London to visit my daughter – and son-in-law. And my husband is almost certain to be made Secretary-General of the IMF.

President Yes, gentlemen, I admit it. I would give my right arm to be Secretary-General.

Education May God grant you your wish!

Health (*aside*) But then there's the question of who gets to take over here.

Finance (*aside*) Now I just have to stop that capitalist pig from taking over.

Justice (*aside*) Secretary-General! It's a joke. Still, it would leave a vacancy at the top here. And this residence is ever so roomy.

Health (*to the President*) Just don't forget your friends, Anton.

Justice Oh, he won't forget to help out old friends in times of difficulty, will you, Anton?

Education My son's trying to get into Columbia next year but he's having trouble on the academic side. You could pull a few strings couldn't you, Anton?

President I'm sure I can.

Anna You're always making promises.

President But my angel, I'm sure I could fit it in.

Anna I'm sure you could, but do you really want to spend time looking after the riff-raff?

Wife (*aside*) Did you hear that? That's how she treats us!

Finance Invite a sow to dinner and she'll crap on your table.

Enter the Head of Intelligence, breathless, holding a printout.

Intelligence Gentlemen. Extraordinary news!

All What? What?

Intelligence Let me just get my breath. The official – (*Pause.*) – we thought was a UN Inspector – (*Pause.*) – wasn't one at all.

All He wasn't the UN Inspector?

Intelligence Not at all. I discovered it in an email.

President You what? (*Beat.*) What email?

Intelligence You know you told me to check all the emails and letters going out of the country for any dissent . . . anyone calling you an idiot or a despot . . .

President Yes yes . . .

Intelligence Well, I ordered a hold to be put on any email containing your name and the words 'fool', 'moron', 'tyrant', 'vicious', 'immoral', 'corrupt, 'genocide' and so on. And this one came up. From Martin Remington Gammon to Scullywag at blueyonder.co.uk. I was terrified. So I opened it.

President You opened an email from him? How dare you?

Intelligence I don't know how! I said to myself, 'Don't open it! Bring it straight to the President,' but the temptation was irresistible. One half of me was going, 'Don't open it or you'll be placed in solitary for the rest of your days,' but the other half was saying, 'Open it, open it.' So I opened it and then everything went dark.

President But how could you even think to open an email from a high-ranking official of the United Nations!

Intelligence But that's the thing. He isn't high-ranking. And he's not from the United Nations.

President Well then, who is he?

Intelligence He's no one. God knows who he is!

President (*heatedly*) What do you mean, he's no one? How dare you call him no one and then say God knows who he is! Arrest this man immediately!

Intelligence Arrest me?

President Yes, you!

Intelligence But Anton, I'm your Chief of Intelligence, you can't arrest me!

President I can do what I like! That man is going to marry my daughter! I am becoming Secretary-General of the United Nations and head of the IMF and you will be rotting in a freezing cell in the coldest corner of the North!

Intelligence Oh Anton, not the North! Let me at least read the email! Please, gentlemen, let me read the email!

All Read it! Read it!

Intelligence (*reads*) 'My dear Scully. I'm dropping you a quick line about a crazy thing that has just happened to me on my travels. As you know I got completely cleaned out by this painter in Tblisi so I arrived in this godforsaken country with not a penny on me. And then, because I looked Western and had an English accent, the entire place mistook me for a UN Inspector. I am currently sitting in the President's personal residence, having a whale of a time, and flirting shamelessly with the President's wife and daughter. Only I couldn't decide who to start with so I thought I'd start with the mum because she seems game for anything. Do you remember when we were stone broke and were squatting in that dodgy council flat in Streatham and we had to steal bread and yams from Brixton market? Well, this is the complete opposite. They're throwing money at me from all directions. They're opening accounts left right and centre. I don't know if you're still thinking of trying to write for *Private Eye* but use this story if you like. I'll fill you in on the details. There's the President . . . a complete turd . . . '

President It can't be! It doesn't say that!

Intelligence Read it yourself!

President (*reads*) 'A complete turd.' It's not possible! You wrote it yourself!

Intelligence How could I have written all that! I don't even know what a turd is!

Health Just read it!

Justice Read it!

Intelligence (*reads*) 'The President, a complete turd . . . '

President Oh, you bastard! Do you have to keep repeating it? As if we hadn't heard it the first time!

Intelligence (*continues reading*) 'Um . . . um . . . um . . . complete turd . . . The Head of Intelligence is quite simply . . . ' Well now, he's not very nice about me.

President Read it. Go on.

Intelligence Well, you get the gist.

President No, if you're going to read it, read it all!

Health If you will allow me. (*Takes the paper, puts on glasses and reads.*) 'The Head of Intelligence is the least intelligent man you are ever likely to meet. I thought Gibson who worked in lettings was bad but compared to this guy he's a genius.'

Intelligence Is that better than 'complete turd'?

Health 'The Minister of Education is very tall.'

Education That's not too bad.

Health 'I think he was breast-fed for too long as a child as he seems to be constantly sucking at an invisible nipple.'

Education I haven't breast-fed for years!

Health 'The Minister of Justice spends most of the time pretending he hasn't got piles.'

Justice The bastard! Who does he think he is?

Health (*continues to read*) 'As for the Minister of Health, Georgy Strawberry . . . um . . . um . . . um . . .'

Finance Why have you stopped?

Health It's suddenly rather hard to read. The ink's faded. Anyway the man's clearly a complete waste of space . . .

Finance Give it to me. I might be able to see better.

Health (*not handing it over*) No, it's just that there's a small passage that's blurry. The next bit's easier.

Intelligence No, read it all!

All Give it to her, Georgy. Come on, 'Strawberry', hand it over!

Health All right! All right! (*He gives her the email.*) There you are (*He covers it with his fingers.*) Read from there.

All No, read it all! Read it all!

Everyone takes a step towards him.

Finance 'The Minister for Health, Georgy Strawberry, is a smarmy little git who seems to think I can help him overthrow the President with American money.'

Health I never said that! No, really, Anton, he's completely misunderstood the drift of what I was saying . . . Let's go on, shall we? (*He grabs the email.*) 'The Minister of Finance offered me even more to keep the Americans away. But she's so ugly I don't think I could ever really side with her.'

Beat.

'That's all I've got time for now, Scully. Hope the novel's progressing. Maybe we could write this up together when I get back, try and flog it to a Sunday. Exclusive exposé. I'll see you in the Dog and Duck Wednesday week for the pub quiz. We can talk about it then. Drinks on me. Martin Remington Gammon.'

Pause.

Wife Well, that's a blow.

President He's torn me apart! He's murdered me! Aaaah! I'm going blind! All I can see is a line of pig snouts! Get him back! Call him back!

Intelligence Some chance of that. Why did I give him the fastest helicopter?

Justice I gave him ten thousand dollars cash!

Education And five thousand from me.

Health Someone catch Stepana, she's about to faint.

President Fuck Stepana! Let her fall! He's got my daughter! My little Maria!

Justice But how could we have made such fools of ourselves?

President How could I, you mean? (*striking his forehead*) I've been in politics for thirty years! I've seen regimes change, generals topple, I've seen the Iron Curtain fall and never has anyone pulled the wool over my eyes! I've never let my opponents get a sniff at the main chance! I rigged three elections! But who cares any more? Being President of this craphouse! Who cares?

Anna But Anton . . . it can't be. He's engaged to little Maria. He's taking her round loft apartments in Mayfair.

President Engaged! Don't you engage me! You can stick your engagement up your arse! (*desperate now*) Go on, gawp away! Take a good look at the idiot you have as a president! A blockhead! A fool! A cretin! (*Brandishes his fist at himself.*) Aaagh, you pug-nosed prick! I took a weedy little toerag for a man of importance. And now he's out of my grasp, flying home eating my honey, snuggling into my rug, fondling my daughter! He'll tell everyone about this. He'll tell the world! It's not enough to be utterly humiliated, he's going to write it all down in some newspaper column. And some other smart-arse Londoner will turn it into a comedy. And all the Londoners with their posh earrings and their low-cut jeans will come and laugh at the thick-headed President and clap their hands! What are you laughing at? You're laughing at yourselves! You're laughing at yourselves! (*He brandishes his fist and stamps his foot. Then stops. Pause. Now quietly.*) Where are they now? I said where are they?

Svistunov They're just about to leave our air space, Mr President.

President Ivan, you stopped the email didn't you? It never reached its destination?

Intelligence That's correct, Anton.

President So no one knows anything yet. It's all on that helicopter.

Anna What are you thinking, Anton?

President If that helicopter doesn't reach its destination, no one will ever be the wiser. A tragic death of a young businessman on his way out of the country.

Anna Anton, you're not suggesting shooting it down?

President Why not? We did it with the leader of the opposition. We reported it as an electrical storm, as I recall.

Dobchinski But Mr President, Maria is in the helicopter.

Pause.

President Aaah! Aaaagh! I can't bear it! I have to kill my own daughter to save my reputation! What kind of sick God invented such a world! Well, it's impossible. Maria is our only daughter.

Anna She's our only daughter.

President Even if the article he writes destroys every single one of us. If the people smash down the gates and lynch us all, and if the few who survive are forced to change their names and wither away their lives in obscure suburban cul-de-sacs, she is still my daughter.

Pause.

Where are they now?

Svistunov They'll leave our air space in five minutes.

Anna What's the weather like?

Svistunov Stormy.

President Just go and check, would you, Svistunov? Those storms in the West can be very unpleasant. Quite lethal sometimes.

Svistunov Is that an order, sir?

President That's an order.

Exit Svistunov. The President laughs.

What did I see in that little pipsqueak that made me think he was even remotely like a UN Inspector? Nothing at all! And suddenly there we all were shouting our heads off: 'It's the UN Inspector. It's the UN Inspector!' Who said it first? Who was it?

Justice (*spreading his arms*) Even if you pointed a gun to my head, I swear I couldn't remember. Some kind of fog descended and we were led astray.

Health I'll tell you who suggested it! Them! (*He points to Dobchinski and Robchinski.*)

Robchinski No, no! It wasn't me! I didn't think . . .

Dobchinski It wasn't anything, it was nothing to do with . . .

Justice But of course! It was you!

Education Yes, I remember! They ran in like madmen yelling, 'He's here, he's here, he's at the Marriott and he's not spending a penny!' We've found the culprits!

President But of course. The spiders. Running around the offices with your endless spinning . . . always spinning . . .

*Everyone surrounds Dobchinski and Robchinski,
laughing.*

Robchinski I swear to God, it wasn't me, it was Peter
Dobchinski . . .

Dobchinski No no, Peter, you were definitely the first to –

Robchinski No, I was not! You were the first!

Dobchinski No, you were!

Robchinski No, you were!

Dobchinski You!

Robchinski You!

Enter Svistunov.

Svistunov Mr President. A violent storm has brought
down the helicopter carrying the British businessman and
your daughter.

President Any survivors?

Svistunov None, sir.

Pause. Anna and the President come together.

President A tragedy.

Justice A tragic accident.

Wife Poor Anna.

Anna So unforeseen.

Education An unforeseen tragedy.

Health An unforeseen tragic event.

President An unforeseen tragic accident. Oh Maria. My
Maria.

Anna My Maria.

President Our Maria.

All Maria. Maria.

They weep together, white hankies out. Collective weeping. Hankies.

Svistunov Sir? On my way to tell you I picked up this memo. (*He pulls out a piece of paper.*) A United Nations Inspector has arrived from New York. He is staying at the Marriott Hotel. He wishes to see you immediately.

His words are like a bolt of lightning. Everyone is struck dumb. The President grabs his heart. The group lets out a collective gasp of astonishment and the hankies gently fall to the ground like snow.

End.